Wendy Craig was born and e[...]
Durham and trained as an actress at the Central
School of Dramatic Art in London. She had her
first big successes at the Royal Court in *A
Resounding Tinkle*, *Sport of My Mad Mother* and
Epitaph for George Dillon. Numerous starring
roles followed in West End plays and television,
and she had an academy nomination for her
performance in the film *The Servant*. She is best
known for her roles on television in *Not in Front
of the Children*, *And Mother Makes Three*, *Butter-
flies* and the much-acclaimed *Nanny*. Her latest
comedy series for the BBC is *Laura and Disorder*.

Wendy Craig has been married for thirty-three
years to journalist, musician and writer, Jack
Bentley. She has two grown-up sons.

In the UK the Save the Children Fund has over
100 projects where work is concentrated in the
inner cities. As well as self-help family centres,
there are programmes for unemployed young-
sters where they can gain new skills and confidence, schemes for disabled children and
projects to help under fives get off to a good
start in life. It also has schemes in some thirty
countries overseas, where projects are developed
to meet local needs. SCF works in collaboration
with governments to establish permanent programmes which will benefit tomorrow's children
as well as today's.

Kids' Stuff

Childhood memories of the famous
collected by Wendy Craig

To Emma
Happy Birthday
Love From
Daniel & Victoria.

_____

FONTANA/Collins

First published in 1988 by Fontana Paperbacks
8 Grafton Street, London W1X 3LA

Printed and bound in Great Britain by
William Collins Sons & Co. Ltd, Glasgow

Foreword
by Wendy Craig

Most of us have vivid memories of our childhood. We recall certain moments, people and places with great clarity and there are particular incidents which we will never forget. Children do strange things sometimes. My early years were spent in a small mining village called Sacriston. It straggled up a steep Durham hill and I can still hear the sound of the 'knocker-up' banging on the back doors of the miners' houses waking them for the early shift. My mother and father were loving, indulgent parents and the only time I saw my father really angry was when a childhood impulse overcame me.

The houses in our street were built of red brick and there was a narrow lane at the back of them for access, where the women hung out their washing. One day, I must have been about five I suppose, I found a tin of bright green gloss paint and a brush in the coal shed. The temptation was too much for me. I crept out into the back lane with it, and liberally loading the brush, I painted a sort of sausage shape on every adjacent red brick wall and wrote underneath it in large print, newly learnt at school, 'The Big Log'. Why I chose this somewhat abstract concept I can't imagine. Anyway, there it was. Awful green graffiti on the walls of a village which had probably never known graffiti before. The neighbours were furious and came rushing round to complain. My guilt was irrefutable. My hands, my clothes, even my hair, were green.

I'd never seen my father so cross. Poor man, he spent ages trying to remove the sticky green murals, but have you ever tried getting gloss paint off rough brick walls?

When I returned to the village twenty years later, I peered at those walls and I swear small blobs of green remained indelibly fixed into the mortar. Now, even when I do anything slightly odd, my husband always says: 'Here we go again . . . "The Big Log".'

This book is filled with childhood eccentricities. It is also a fascinating insight into the formative years of many famous people. For instance, who would imagine that the Duke of Bedford brought up in grand houses against a background of opulence would regard his childhood with loathing, that Bob Hoskins screamed because he wasn't allowed to wear a party dress, or that Bruce Kent was stricken with guilt at the age of eight because he thought he had committed adultery.

I found that reading the responses was totally compulsive and often hilarious and I am deeply indebted to everyone who gave of their time and energy to this project. People are so generous, and I feel it's particularly true of busy people.

Anyway, I thank them all warmly for sharing these special memories in order to enrich the lives of children who are less fortunate.

Sir Hugh Casson, CH KCVO PPRA RDI

Firsts

Childhood is inevitably a series of 'Firsts' recalled more by smells and sounds than by sights . . . the first ecstasy or humiliation . . . the first visit to London (Ah, Selfridges!) or the sea (the stretching sands and full circle horizons of Dymchurch) . . . the first failure (in the gym), the first success (in the art room), the first death (the family collie swathed in an old pair of my combinations lying stiffly behind the compost heap) . . . the first fight, the first publicly shed blood (a dried pool outside the door of Hythe Church the morning after a Gotha raid in 1916 or thereabouts. We had slept the previous night under my Aunt's grand-piano while the bombs thudded down) . . . the first time a telephone was used (to speak to my mother announcing the time of my arrival at Folkestone) . . . the first treason (I had promised to look after a young cousin newly arrived at school. I ignored him) . . . the first school cap to be thrown – like John Betjeman's – over the hedge by jeering companions.

On the whole, more distress than pleasure is what survives from early days . . . and how long ago in retrospect they seem today and how secret were one's enthusiasms and interests and how wonderfully selfish.

David Shilling

I'm not yet at that stage where policemen look young. A few traffic wardens do, but then they are, aren't they? But I have noticed how grown-up kids are nowadays. I suppose I was too when I was younger. Happily my schooldays weren't the happiest days of my life – and many childish treats are more special now. I'll admit, I love ice cream, Marmite on toast, peanut butter with jam, comics, Care Bears; and no school and no exams! Even spinach tastes good now, Shakespeare, rhubarb and walking have all improved. No wonder an interviewer recently asked me what I wanted to do when I grew up!

Of course my childhood was fortunate, but many aren't. What one mustn't forget is, however grown-up kids appear – however strong in the school playground, each and every one is frightfully vulnerable. So it's especially vital to help a child when you can – on the whole they are unable to help themselves.

Henry Cooper, OBE KSG

When I was at school, I wasn't a very good scholar as I was always interested in sport. It is only later in life that one realizes that you should study more at school, because education is the greatest thing in life.

Penelope Fitzgerald

Children's misunderstandings are often the understandings which grown-ups once had, but have forgotten. Then they act, quite unconsciously, as a reproach.

The artist George Morrow told me that he was once out sketching with a friend on a strand in the West of Ireland. I say 'sketching', but in fact the two of them were working hard, making accurate studies of clouds and gulls and the bits and pieces on the foreshore. A child, looking tiny in the distance, approached gradually over the long shining beach. George said he didn't look much bigger when he got close to them. He had his boots tied together by their laces and hung round his neck, and he stopped to look at what they were doing. Like most small children he was fascinated by the drawings which were 'just like'. He asked no questions, simply nodded and stared. But artists, on the whole, are not fascinated by being stared at.

'Get him to go away,' said George's friend.

'Where to?'

'He must have come from somewhere.'

George took out a sixpence. 'Take that and go and buy some sweets.'

The child took the money and departed. Far away

they could see him turn off the strand where the track ran down to the coast and sit down to put his boots on, to walk to heaven knows where.

They went on working for perhaps an hour and a half, until the late afternoon light was levelling across the sea.

'My God, there he is again,' said George. 'You'd think once would be enough for one day.'

They began to walk to the other end of the strand, so fast that the little boy, although he had started to run, had no hope of catching up with them. Still, for a young child he had remarkable determination. In the end they stopped, not having the heart to go on. He came up with them, panting and half sobbing, with a paper bag held aloft.

'Here's your sweets, mister, and here's your penny change.'

George knew better than to give him the sweets. He gave him his sketchbook.

Baroness Masham of Ilton

When my two children were young, I employed a woman to drive them to school and help. She herself had a little black boy who was both deaf and unable to speak. This little boy was two – he had a peripatetic teacher who used to come and visit and I always felt she supported and did more for the mother than actually having much effect on the child.

My two children who were older used to take him out into the garden and play with him – they used to swing him on the swing just as they would any other child, and his face would break into a wonderful smile and he would roar with laughter.

The only time I really saw him motivated and full of the joy of life was when he was playing with my two children.

I sometimes think that children can bring on the multiply handicapped better than anyone else, because they treat them in the same way as other children. Parents are so often overprotective and worried about them and forget that they need to be children and to enjoy the thrills and spills of life just the same as anyone else.

General Eva Burrows
General, The Salvation Army

Jesus doesn't know the difference

Working as a teacher on a mission station in Zimbabwe, I was training the small children to act a nativity play at Christmas time. They were almost all black children, but of the eight angels two were little blonde girls, the daughters of Norwegian missionaries.

At the dress rehearsal, I was standing behind the scenery ready to redirect any of the angels who got confused in the heavenly chorus. They looked delightful in their white robes, with tinselled haloes and shiny wings. During a lull in the proceedings, I saw one of the little Norwegians looking at the other angels with a puzzled air. Then she turned to her sister, and in a stage whisper said, 'Bertha, do you think there will be black angels in Heaven?'

To which the older sister replied in an exasperated tone, 'Of course there will. Anyhow Jesus doesn't know the difference.'

Camilla Jessel Panufnik, FRPS
Photographer for The Save the Children Fund

Njoroge Whittington

What, I wonder, has become of Njoroge? I met him in 1963 at SCF's Nairobi Rescue Centre, where he was reigning jester and soloist in the frequent sing-songs. I'm still haunted by the firm intent and intelligence in his wide, dark eyes – childish, yet old through suffering and unquenchable will-power. If he's not yet prime minister, I can't help imagining that he's at least the equivalent of lord mayor.

Coming from a remote village, he was lucky to have briefly sampled education; but when he was eleven, his father left home and no-one could pay the school fees.

Njoroge had heard that the streets of Nairobi were

paved with gold. He walked, without food, more than 200 miles to the city, clutching only a modest-sized basket to carry home the gold. However, the pavements were dark and dusty and, like thousands of other boy vagrants lured by similar tales of riches and learning, then forced by hunger into robbing dustbins, he was rounded up by harassed police and unkindly bundled home on a lorry.

Njoroge ran away to Nairobi again, was repatriated and returned to Nairobi – twelve times! His passion to be educated outweighed the agony of extreme hunger and punitive beatings, the misery of rags, filth and sleeping in gutters. He would never give up, though the tangles with the police were a nightmare! Fortunately, gossip along the gutter-line finally led him to a Rescue Centre for vagrant boys run by SCF, and his dream of education became reality.

Can anyone tell me, where is Njoroge now?

Claire Rayner

Lost child

I shall call her Barbara, Busia in Polish, her native tongue. It is not her real name, you understand; she is a very private person and would be mortified if I told you that. And I shall call him Henry, which is not his real name either. So, Barbara and Henry, happy in an ordinary sort of way, just part of a family, the way people are.

Until the Germans came to their town of Lublin in Poland. What year was it? Who can say? 1937, perhaps, or '38. When you are quiet and happy and busy with the babies, who counts the years? They took Barbara and her babies, including Henry, not yet old enough for school, a clever funny bouncy little boy, and put them all in concentration camps. 'Arbeit macht frei' it said over the entrance, but Henry couldn't read, so he didn't work. And what work could a boy of four or five do anyway? His bigger sisters and brothers couldn't work either, so they disappeared just as his father did. Henry never knew where they went. Barbara, his mother, knew, but she didn't say.

And then it was 1946 and suddenly it was all different. Henry still hadn't been to school, although now he was eleven years old. Couldn't read, couldn't write, thin as a rake, all eyes and teeth, really. But alive, like Barbara. Just the two of them alive. There had been more but Henry couldn't remember now who they had been and how many. Just father and the others – but all gone now.

Oh, the excitement when the gates under the sign 'Arbeit macht frei' opened! Oh, the tears and the running and the hoping! But perhaps Henry ran too fast or Barbara wasn't looking clearly, through her tears . . . anyway they lost each other. Hundreds of thousands of lost people wandering around Europe, herded into new camps – not concentration camps, but camps all the same, as distracted officials tried to sort them out, find them homes and jobs and a new life away from a Europe so devastated by its war that it could barely breathe.

And in the middle of it all, Henry, lost. Barbara looking for Henry, lost in a camp somewhere. But what camp? Where had the distracted officials taken Henry when Barbara wasn't watching? There was only one way to find out, so Barbara did it.

She walked. She walked from Poland to Germany. From Germany to Czechoslovakia. From Czechoslovakia to Hungary. From Hungary to Austria. Hundreds – no thousands – of miles on her own two feet. Walking from camp to camp, asking if they had a boy there called Henry, her Henry, a lost child. And in each camp the distracted officials clucked sympathetically and looked in their records and shook their tired heads and regretted, so sorry, can't help. Try Camp number seventy-seven, only three hundred miles away, try seventy-seven, or seventy-eight, or seventy-nine . . .

Eighteen months, walking and walking, and getting her food where she could, Barbara looking for lost Henry. And then at last making the last journey, from Austria to Italy. The last camp, the end of her road. If Henry wasn't there, she would have to stop looking, stop walking. She would grieve for him, and know that all her family had gone. The last camp, and the last child.

She sat in the commandant's office on a hot Italian morning, the sun patterning the wooden floor, and asked for news of Henry. Had they such a child of such a name? The official, the most distracted she had ever met yet (*very* Italian, thought Barbara privately), looked in his records and shook his head. No child called Henry on his books. And Barbara sat by the open window and wept for her lost Henry, not here in the last camp of all.

A boy outside who had been bouncing his ball – the only possession he had, but that is another story – against

15

the window frame, looked in through the window at the crying woman.

'Did I hear you say you were looking for Henry?' he said in a conversational sort of way, bouncing his ball against the frame as he spoke. 'I know him. He lives in my hut . . .' And he took her down the long alley ways between the huts and there was Henry, playing soccer with a bundle of tied-up rags for a ball.

That's all there is to the story, really. Barbara and Henry were sent to Canada on a refugee ship and there, at the age of almost thirteen, Henry at last went to school. He learned to read and write, to count and think, and worked so hard and so fast that he was awarded a degree in biochemistry at the University of Montreal when he was only a couple of years older than the other students in his year who had been at school since they were five and who had never walked under signs that said 'Arbeit macht frei' and who had never been lost. He grew up to be a clever funny bouncy sort of man, who smiles a lot and laughs easily. And one day he met and married my – but I can't tell you that because Henry is like his mother, Barbara. A private sort of person who would be mortified if I told you more.

Bill Naughton

The Facts of Life – 1930 and 1985 versions
(From a journal of conversations written down exactly as told)

1930

'I remember like it was yesterday the first time I was told the facts of life – where babies come from,' said Mona, a woman born in Bolton, 'I mean it came as such a shock to me. I must have been about nine at the time – yes, nine, nineteen-thirty it was, when they brought in the Means Test for the unemployed. I was with this pal of mine, a girl called Alice Adams, a year or two older than me, and she an' myself were wheelin' this pram, with two or three younger children in tow as well. That's what you did in those days – you'd just go to a door of any woman who had had a baby an' ask could you wheel the carriage – as it was called – round the street. If they had one – an' many homes didn't – they'd be glad to let you wheel it for an hour or two. An' for us it was a lot better than playin' with dolls. Anyway, as we were walking along the street, with this baby in the pram, Alice, who must have only heard recently herself, began telling me that babies aren't brought in the midwife's bag – an' went on with all the horrible details. I was right shocked for a minute or two, then suddenly I stopped the pram in the street, faced up to her, and said,

"I know for certain positive, Alice Adams, that what you're tellin' me can't be true!"

"Oh, an' how do you know for certain positive that it can't be true?" she said, "Our Royal Family," I said, "that's how I know." "What about our Royal Family?" she said. "They've had five or six children, haven't they?' I said. "Yes," she said. "What about it?" "Well, you're not standin' there, Alice Adams," I said to her, "tryin' to tell me when their majesties retire of a night, that King George an' Queen Mary start mankin' about with one another like that in bed! Because nob'dy in their right mind will believe a tale like that!"'

1985

Mavis and Harry, a couple in their seventies, Lancastrians, were having tea with us, 'Last Saturday night,' said Harry, 'our granddaughter Sandra was stayin' with us – she's just turned seven but if her Mum an' Dad are goin' out she likes to come to us. Anyway, we were chattin' about our Johnny's twenty-first birthday party – there's a long gap between brother and sister – an' it'll be in August, an' they're layin' on a good do. Anyway, Sandra suddenly says to me, "Grandpa, how long were my Mum an' Dad married before they had our Johnny?" So I said, "Oh a long time, musta been years." Didn't I, Mavis?' Then Mavis took up the story at that point: 'Yes,' she said, 'Harry said, "Years – " an' just waved his hand, y'know, tryin' to shut her up. But Sandra had been reckoning up, and she said, "Mum an' Dad celebrated twenty-one years of being married in January, didn't they?" An' I said, "Yes, what about it?" An' she said, "Which means they must have been married in January nineteen-sixty-four, eh?" An' I said, "Yes." An' she

18

went on, "An' our Johnny was born in August." So Harry said, "Well, what about it? – I don't know what you're goin' on about." An' our Sandra grinned across to me, "We know – don't we, Nana!" she said. An' do you know she couldn't stop smiling to herself and nodding across at me, an' lookin' at Harry there, as though he were a bit soft in the head.'

Tim Pigott-Smith

One of the teachers to whom I shall remain always indebted was the man who first put me into plays. He was, in fact, the history teacher – Ed Raynor – and he still teaches at my old grammar school in Leicester, although that school is now a sixth form college.

I have always remained in touch with him – he is an ebullient lively-minded man who enjoys life greatly, and always took great pride in his pupils, holding up his past successes to us when we were young as shining examples of what we might achieve, if we got down to it. I imagine that his task was simpler then than it is now, that society made it easier to offer young people trustworthy incentives – a time of hope rather than a time of cynicism, a time of just reward rather than a time of self-service.

The last time I saw Ed, we walked together round the old school buildings; two Indian boys were playing badminton in the old Great Hall – no longer used for assembly, or for those school plays we had done together.

The magnificent old organ in the balcony at the rear of the hall, was, it seemed, rarely if ever, played now, although in my mind I could still hear the organ-scholars thundering away on it. My past was less linked with this building than Ed's and it may be that the values that have replaced ours are fairer, but feeling the tug of nostalgia as strongly as I did for those optimistic days of my lost schooling, I could only imagine how intense was the sense of loss that Ed felt, and how admirable the dignity with which he continued to serve the school he still loves, and the pupils he assists with such selfless dedication.

'The thing is, Tim,' he said, 'they are only with me for two years now. I never get to know them. In your time, a boy was with me for five years minimum, and the history specials for seven!'

His loyalty to the school now would not let him say more than that. But his understatement spoke volumes. It did so again when we visited the headmaster's house. This had been in my day, a place of wonder and respect, a symbol of the value and power of the headmaster; he himself had never been a remote man, calling me by name from my first year – not bad in a school of over one thousand boys. 'Can we go in now?' I asked as we approached. Twenty-five years before, we would never have dreamt of going through the gate, the possibility of actually going through the door as well, had never before occurred to me. That was almost hallowed ground! Ed showed me in.

The smell of gymnasium greeted me. Broken down lockers stood in what I imagined had been the hall – now a kind of cloakroom area. Bits of kit, rulers and exercise books were around us, peeping out of bags and half-open locker doors. There were several class-room doors leading to other areas of the 'house'.

Ed pointed . . .

'That was the lounge, through there . . . and when headmaster entertained,' (Ed always referred to him as just 'headmaster'), 'this is where we used to dine, here in the hall.' With a vigorous pleasure and an enthusiasm brought on by the memory, he continued . . . 'We had some marvellous evenings here, Tim. When we had had dinner headmaster used to clear the table away and we would all dance . . .'

In my mind's eye I could see them, the men who had taught me, twirling, spinning, talking and laughing in their mysterious leisure hours with their wives and girlfriends, ghosts of my former days suddenly made real as people to me by this off-duty image of them. Perhaps some of the people who are lucky enough to be taught by Ed realize their luck at the time – a Mr Chips should be a thing of the present. I never thought of Ed as Mr Chips then, but I do now: it's too late for me, but for somebody else, it may not be.

Bishop of Bath and Wells

An RI teacher friend of mine in a church primary school, and very keen on wildlife, took her class one spring into one of the woods managed by the Somerset Trust for Nature Conservation. The children had a lovely time, following nature trails, listening to the birds, watching the nesting boxes etc. At the end of the morning she got the class together, very happy herself, and the children bubbling with delight at it all. 'Now let's thank God, boys and girls, for all that we've seen and done out in the open air today. Is there something special that any of you would like to pray about?' After a silence, a six year old piped up: 'Yes, Miss, thank you, God, for such a lovely tree to wee-wee behind.'

David Lodge

The Miser

After the War there was a terrible shortage of fireworks. During the War there hadn't been any fireworks at all; but that was because of the blackout, and because the fireworks-makers were making bombs instead. When the War ended everybody said all the pre-war things, like fireworks, would come back. But they hadn't.

Timothy's mother said the rationing was disgraceful, and his father said they wouldn't catch him voting Labour again, but fireworks weren't even rationed. Rationing would have been fair, anyway, even if it was only six each, or say twelve. Twelve different ones. But there just weren't any fireworks to be had, unless you were very lucky. Sometimes boys at school brought them in, and let off the odd banger in the bogs, for a laugh.

They spoke vaguely of getting them 'down the Docks', or from a friend of their dad's, or from a shop that had discovered some pre-war stock, and sold out the same day.

Timothy and Drakey and Woppy had searched all over the neighbourhood for such a shop. Once they did find a place advertising fireworks, but when the man brought them out they were all the same kind, bangers. You couldn't have a proper Guy Fawkes' Night with just bangers. Besides, they weren't one of the proper makes, like Wells, Standard, or Payne's. They were called 'Whizzo', and had a suspiciously home-made look about them. They cost tenpence each, which was a shocking price to charge for bangers. In the end they bought two each and, with only three weeks to go before November the Fifth, that was still their total stock.

One day Timothy's mother set his heart leaping when she came in from shopping and announced that she had got some fireworks for him. But when she produced them they were only the sparkler things that you held in your hand – little kids' stuff. He'd been so sulky that in the end his mother wouldn't let him have the sparklers, which he rather regretted afterwards.

None of them, not even Drakey, who was the oldest, had a clear memory of Guy Fawkes' Night before the War. But they all remembered VJ Night, when there was a bonfire on the bomb-site in the middle of the street where the flying-bomb had fallen, and the sky was gaudy with rockets, and a man from one of the houses at the end of the street had produced two whole boxes of super fireworks, saying he'd saved them for six years for this night. The next morning Timothy had roamed the bomb-site and collected all the charred cases as, in previous years, he had collected shrapnel. That was when he had first learned the haunting names – 'Chrysanthemum Fire,' 'Roman Candle', 'Volcano', 'Silver Rain', 'Torpedo', 'Moonraker' – beside which the 'Whizzo Banger' struck a false and unconvincing note.

One Saturday afternoon Timothy, Drakey and Woppy wandered far from their home ground, searching for fireworks. The best kind of shop was the kind that sold newspapers, sweets, tobacco and a few toys. They found several new ones, but had no luck. Some of the shops even had notices in the window: 'No Fireworks'.

'If they had any,' said Drakey bitterly, 'I bet they wouldn't sell them. They'd keep them for their own kids.'

'Let's go home,' said Woppy. 'I'm tired.'

On the way home they played 'The Lost Platoon', a game based on a serial story in Drakey's weekly comic. Drakey was Sergeant McCabe, the leader of the platoon, Timothy was Corporal Kemp, the quiet, clever one, and Woppy was 'Butch' Baker, the strong but rather stupid private. The platoon was cut off behind enemy lines and the game consisted in avoiding the observation of Germans. Germans were anyone who happened to be passing.

'Armoured vehicles approaching,' said Timothy.

Drakey led them into the driveway of a private golf course. They lay in some long grass while two women with prams passed on the pavement. Timothy glanced idly round him, and sat up sharply.

'Look!' he breathed, scarcely able to believe such luck. About thirty yards away, on some rough ground screened from the road by the golf-club fence, was a ramshackle wooden shed. Leaning against one wall was

24

a notice, crudely painted on a wooden board. 'Fireworks for Sale', it said.

Slowly they got to their feet and, with silent, wondering looks at each other, approached the shed. The door was open, and inside an old man was sitting at a table, reading a newspaper and smoking a pipe. A faded notice over his head said: 'Smoking Prohibited'. He looked up and took the pipe out of his mouth.

'Yes?' he said.

Timothy looked for help to Drakey and Woppy, but they were just gaping at the man and at the dusty boxes piled on the floor.

'Er . . . you haven't any fireworks, have you?' Timothy ventured at last.

'Yes, I've got a few left, son. Want to buy some?'

The fireworks were sold loose, not in pre-packed boxes, which suited them perfectly. They took a long time over their selection, and it was dark by the time they had spent all their money. On the way home they stopped under each lamp-post to open their paper bags and reassure themselves that their treasure was real. The whole episode had been like a dream, or a fairy tale, and Timothy was afraid that at any moment the fireworks would dissolve.

As they reached the corner of their street, Timothy said: 'Whatever you do, don't tell anybody where we got them.'

'Why?' said Woppy.

'So that we can go back and get some more, before he sells out.'

'I've spent all my fireworks money anyway,' said Drakey.

'Yes, but it's ages to Guy Fawkes, and we've got pocket money to come,' argued Timothy.

But when they went back the following Saturday, the shed was locked, and the notice was gone. They peered through the windows, but there was only dusty furniture to be seen.

'Must have sold out,' said Drakey. But there was something creepy about the sudden disappearance of the fireworks man, and they hurried away from the shed and never spoke of it again.

Each evening, as soon as he got home from school, Timothy got out the box in which he had put his fireworks and counted them. He took them all out and arranged them, first according to size, then according to type, then according to price. He pored over the brightly-coloured labels, studying intently the blurred instructions: *hold in a gloved hand, place in earth and stand well back, nail to a wooden post.* He handled the fireworks with great care, grudging every grain of gunpowder that leaked out and diminished the glory to come.

'I wonder you keep those things under your bed,' said his mother. 'Remember what happened to the sweets.'

About a year previously, an American relative had sent Timothy a large box of 'candies', as she called them. Their bright wrappings and queer names – *Oh Henry!*, *Lifesavers* and *Baby Ruth* – had fascinated him much as the fireworks did; and he was so overwhelmed by the sense of his own wealth amid universal sweet-rationing that he had hoarded them under his bed and ate them sparingly. But they had started to go mouldy, and attracted mice, and his mother threw them away.

'Mice don't eat fireworks,' he said to her, stroking the

stick of his largest rocket. But on second thoughts, he asked his mother to keep them for him in a warm, dry cupboard.

'How d'you know they'll go off, anyway?' said his father. 'Pre-war, aren't they? Probably dud by now.'

Timothy knew his father was teasing, but he took the warning seriously. 'We'll have to try one,' he said solemnly to Drakey and Woppy, 'To see if they're all right. We'd better draw lots.'

'I don't mind letting off one of mine,' said Drakey.

'No, I want to let off one of mine,' said Woppy.

In the end, they let off one each. Woppy chose a 'Red Flare', and Drakey a 'Roman Candle'. Timothy couldn't understand why they didn't let off the cheapest ones. They went to the bomb-site to let them off. For a few dazzling seconds the piles of rubble, twisted iron, planks and rusty water cisterns were illuminated with garish colour. When it was over they blinked in the dim light of the street-lamps and grinned at each other.

'Well, they work all right,' said Drakey.

The other two tried to persuade Timothy to let off one of his. He was tempted, but he knew he would regret it later, and refused. They quarrelled, and Drakey taunted Timothy with being a Catholic like Guy Fawkes. Timothy said that he didn't care, that you didn't have to be against Guy Fawkes to have fireworks, and that he wasn't interested in the Guy part anyway. He went home alone, got out his fireworks, and sat in his bedroom all the evening, counting and arranging them.

Once Drakey and Woppy had broken into their store, they could not restrain themselves till November the Fifth. They started with one firework a night, then it went up to two, then it was three. Drakey had a talent for discovering new and spectacular ways of using them. He would drop a lighted banger into an old water tank and produce an explosion that brought the neighbours to their doors, or he would shoot a 'Torpedo' out of a length of drain-pipe. Timothy had a few ideas of his own, but, as he stubbornly refused to use any of his own fireworks, the most he could ask was to be a passive spectator. His turn would come on November the Fifth, when the empty-handed Drakey and Woppy would be glad to watch his display.

On the evening of November 4th, Timothy counted his collection for the last time.

'You'll be lost without those things after tomorrow,' said his mother.

'I don't believe he really wants to set them off,' said his father.

''Course I do,' said Timothy. But he closed the lid of the box with a sigh.

'I'll be glad to see the back of them, anyway,' said his mother. 'Now, who could that be?'

His father answered the door. The policeman was so big he seemed to fill the entire room. He smiled encouragingly at Timothy, but Timothy just hugged his box to his chest, and looked at his feet.

'Look, Sergeant,' said his father, 'I realize that if these fireworks are really stolen goods – '

'Not exactly stolen, sir,' said the policeman, 'But as good as. This old codger just broke into the storage shed and set up shop.'

'Well, what I mean is, I know you're entitled to take them away, but this is a special case. You know what kids are like about fireworks. He's been looking forward to Guy Fawkes' Night for weeks.'

'I know, sir, I've got kids myself. But I'm sorry. This is the only lot we've been able to trace. We'll need them for evidence.' He turned to Timothy. 'D'you happen to know, sonny, if any of your friends bought fireworks off the same man?'

Timothy nodded speechlessly, trying not to cry. 'But I'm the only one that saved them,' he said: and with the words the tears rolled uncontrollably down his cheeks.

Robin Cousins

I was on the ice offering advice to a class of eager school children and whilst showing one child how to execute a specific movement, another small six year old grabbed my sweatshirt saying 'I do it this way' and proceeded to show me. I watched her and she grinned enthusiastically, but when I started to correct an error and offer guidance by saying, 'You should . . .' she stopped me in my tracks with: '*I* said, *this* is how *I* do it', and skated off leaving me wondering if I had just encountered the first DIY skating star!

John Sparkes

I think that if I remembered anything at all about my childhood I would go mad straight away. But here's some stuff about Siadwel: I know him very well. He dictated this.

'I grew up to be a boy and I used to go to school quite a lot. I was very popular there. Everyone liked flushing my head down the toilet.

We used to do school plays and I would get quite unusual parts. One year we did "A Christmas Carol" by Charles Dickens and I had to be the Smell of Christmas Past. Another year we did "Babes in the Wood" and I had to be Leaf Mould. Somebody had to do it.

Sometimes we'd get a visit from the blind school dentist. He'd feel our teeth in the morning and tune the piano in the afternoon. The headmaster would talk to us before he came. He would say, "Dentist Bowen is coming today. You all know the drill. No screaming and put those sweets away where he can't hear them."

He only recognized people by their teeth. He'd come up to you in the street and say, "Hullo, Siadwel," and you could never say anything back because his hand was in your mouth. It was difficult to have a conversation with him.

Because of the NHS cuts they couldn't afford to give him a guide dog to start with. He had to have a guide rabbit. But everyone got fed up with digging him out of rabbit holes all the time. He got a guide dog in the end. Part time. The rest of the time he had to make do with shouting, "Where am I?"

We'd get school reports. The best one I had said, "Siadwel is more intelligent than a tree." I liked that.

I didn't like Gary Price though. He was a very evil boy who came from a broken home which he had broken himself. He was very disappointed when he found out that having a police record prevents you joining the police. He'd thought you couldn't join if you didn't have one.

He used to laugh at my flared underpants when we got changed for gym, which was our PE teacher's name. Jim used to like to hit my head with his hand and say, "Siadwel, why are you so stupid?" One day I said, "Perhaps it's because you keep hitting my head." He didn't know what to say to that. So he hit me again. I suppose that's why they call it physical education. I can't remember any more after that.'

Lady Alexandra Metcalfe
Vice-President, The Save the Children Fund

I was always mad about dogs and at last my father agreed that I should have one. An extraordinary number of dogs were brought along to the house for his approval. Finally a small Pomeranian arrived. It was not a good looking dog, but when it lifted its leg on one of the Foreign Office Boxes which my father had brought home, he decided that it showed initiative. So we chose Bobby, who became my beloved dog and stayed with me for the rest of his life.

Prue Leith

A friend left a new baby-sitter with a brand new two-way baby alarm for listening to the children from the sitting room. Hearing the eldest child cough the baby-sitter spoke to him through the machine: 'Felix, are you all right?' No answer. 'Felix, are you OK?' Three-year-old Felix finally answered a little hesitantly, 'Hullo wall.'

The Rt. Hon. Mrs Lynda Chalker
Member of Parliament

When I was about nine years old, my father, who was a leading councillor in our Borough, decided that campaigning tactics were the only way to prevent the building of a multistorey block of flats in a local beauty spot.

Leaflets and a petition were prepared for all the homes in the vicinity. It was glorious weather and an ideal time to be out and about. It was my task to help deliver and collect all the leaflets and notices. So I began my first step in learning about local environment campaigns. To me it was fun doing my rounds on my bicycle, but it also taught me about consulting people and campaigning. The local meeting we held was, I am told, unanimous

34

that there should be no building on the cliff. To this day, thankfully none has been built.

Naomi Mitchison

It is doubly necessary to encourage little girls to do wild and dangerous things because they will find too many kind people who will fuss over them and try to stop them. My mother was before her time in allowing and even encouraging me to play dangerously. We used to go on holiday to Cornwall – in those days Sennen, now a tourist centre, was a fishing village. We were only there because my father, in the course of his work, had to be near the Cornish tin mines; they called him The Doctor down in Sennen Cove and, although it was many years since he had changed from medicine to science, he had to set bones and give what medicines he could get. Meanwhile, my mother let me walk along the cliffs above Land's End, knowing I had no fear of heights – that came years later – climb anything climbable and cling to rocks as the sea came raging in. But it was all right. Sometimes I had a wave over my head, but I kept a good grip. The fishermen took me out to the Longships Lighthouse when they took over the rations. One of them would throw me off the boat to be caught in the arms of a lighthouse man.

But we didn't have guns and I don't think my brother and I ever played soldiers in the all too realistic way children do now. But of course we had forts in prickly hedges. Fireworks were not so large and lethal in those days and we looked forward to them. Failing real fireworks we emptied cartridges and made volcanoes or, once, an explosion large enough to break the kitchen window – what fun that was! And of course we were always falling into the river – the Cherwell, not as dirty in those days as it is now – and swimming away from anyone trying to rescue us.

I tried to encourage my own children to do dangerous things but clearly I failed as they now remember only the things I wouldn't let them do. But I do remember seeing two of them climbing across the face of our London house – three storeys up – and carefully keeping my mouth shut. Obviously danger is something very attractive and with luck one may go very near and relish the excitement and the certainty that one can cope, and do this over and over again. And never reach the nasty point when one's luck fails. Never.

Leslie Crowther

Like most boys, I developed the usual healthy interest in the opposite sex. I spent hours wondering what they looked like without their clothes on. The fact that one could see little girls wandering about in local paddling pools, or by the seaside, stark naked, was unimpressive. They were only toddlers, so they didn't count! It was one's contemporaries at school that one mentally stripped in the playground.

I had my first break at the age of eight, when a nubile young lady of the same age – or maybe she was a year or two older – virtually picked me up in the school holidays, and invited herself round for tea. My mother suggested that we should go upstairs and play in my bedroom after tea; a suggestion that Deirdre Bosworth seized upon eagerly. You see, I even remember her name! Once upstairs, she offered me a tour of inspection. Breathlessly I accepted her offer, and she divested herself of her blouse and vest. 'Those are called breasts,' she declared. I was not impressed. I'd seen fat boys in the showers who were bigger than she was!

This is probably why, when I was twelve and at a co-educational school in Twickenham, I evolved *my plan*. Not only were the girls of my age infinitely shapelier by then, but we all used to go to the same public swimming baths for swimming lessons. Our changing rooms were divided by a wooden screen which started at the ceiling but didn't quite reach the ground. I bought a pocket mirror and instructed my mates to do the same. At the next opportunity, we placed the mirrors in a row on the floor under the screen which divided us from the girls, and by skilfully tilting them we saw the lot!

The following week we were surprised to hear sounds of uncontrolled mirth coming from the other side of the screen. Staring aghast at the floor, we saw a row of mirrors tilted towards us. It wasn't their retaliation that rankled – it was their laughter!

Mind you, it was a very cold day!

Mike Yarwood OBE

One of my most vivid childhood memories was performing on the top of an air raid shelter at the bottom of our garden.

At a very early age I always had the urge to be elevated on to anything that would represent a stage. Many is the time I would hold concerts in the garden and perform for my friends, a captive audience, as the garden gate was locked!

Eventually the Council demolished the air raid shelter, fortunately I wasn't appearing on it at the time!

Tam Dalyell

Member of Parliament

A man in a vast sombrero hat, with bushy whiskers came often to our house. He was Australian. I came to think he was marvellous. He used to tell me spine-chilling stories every time he visited. Only later, did I discover that the late Professor Gordon Childe was one of the greatest anthropologists of the century. I guess I owe him my abiding interest in ancient civilization.

For 21 years, I have been the weekly Westminster columnist of *New Scientist*. My interest was ignited by

another visitor to our house, a German, of precise manner, daunting to some adults, but charming to children. How he could explain things like light and the sun's heat to children! I thought he knew more than my teachers. Probably he did. For he was Professor Max Born, then at Edinburgh University, one of the prime movers in ushering in the atomic age.

In my father and mother, and their range of friends, I was extremely privileged.

Ernie Wise

I can remember appearing at a concert in the Yorkshire town of Morley. It was a talent contest and I won first prize of five pounds. I was about nine at the time. At the end of the show we lined up to collect our prizes. Mine was in an envelope in cash. The third prize was a big box of Black Magic chocolates. I can still remember thinking at the time I would much rather have the third prize!

I also remember as a little boy of nine appearing in the Working Men's Clubs with my father. In those days we did a double act called 'Carson and Kid'.

One club I appeared at I remember vividly. I did my clog dance on a billiard table, and during the course of the evening, they had a raffle. The prize was a budgerigar in a cage, which I would have loved to have taken home with me. You see, I've always loved children and animals. I won't appear with them on stage, but I love them.

Needless to say I did not win the budgerigar in a cage, but seeing my obvious disappointment they promised me one the next year when I returned to the club. So, with great anticipation I waited all year for my budgerigar in the cage. The great day arrived and we returned to the club. I did my clog dance on the billiard table. They did not forget and they presented me with the bird. I was overjoyed. I took it home that night and hung it in my bedroom.

The following morning, I didn't like seeing the bird within the confines of a cage so I let it out so it could fly about the bedroom.

I went into the bathroom to clean my teeth. Meanwhile my mother came into my bedroom to make the bed and she opened the window to let some fresh air into the room. That's the last I saw of my budgerigar – his name was 'Charlie'.

Altogether, Aaahhhhhhh.

Rabbi Lionel Blue

Divine dating

He used to pay a call upon my mother's parents in Stepney every Sabbath afternoon. He wore a frock coat and a high hat and in his hand he carried a large red umbrella. This he held like a bishop's crook, for its presence was not a sign of impending rain but of forthcoming marriages. It was his sign of office, the insignia of his profession. He was the local marriage broker. His reception matched his status. He was ushered into the parlour, not the kitchen, and only the best tea set was good enough for him.

My mother's parents had discussed his visit the whole week, and they sat stiffly on either side of him, grandma trying to look a lady (which she was) and grandpa trying to look pious (which he wasn't).

All the young people in the family were introduced to him, like débutantes being presented at court, and even I, though still a child, was not missed out. I was a long term investment and had to be hauled out from under the bed.

Gravely, their prospects were discussed. There was a possible match with the girl round the corner. Her piety made up for her pimples.

He shook his head sadly over the dowries my grandparents could provide, saved up in a slump from household pennies. He didn't think he could get our girl a real tailor, or a cutter. A factory hand perhaps – an older man, of course, but kind!

This was how they were married off. There was no compulsion but romantic love was frowned upon as indecent. Only an arranged marriage was respectable and likely to last.

When the young couple were introduced I was grabbed from the street, washed, scrubbed and unwillingly appointed chaperone. The young people (often in their thirties) paraded slowly down Whitechapel High Street, and I brought up the rear. I was six years old but already a guardian of decency. No wonder I became a minister, after this training. If my unmarried aunt went out for tea, she stood in the doorway of the teashop and solemnly counted the number of men and the number of women. If the former outnumbered the latter, I was sent for to protect her honour. I was bribed with pastries.

It was such a pure world – an adjective scarcely understood now. Over every brass matrimonial bedstead hung the occupants' marriage contract, framed in gilt, to show whoever dared to doubt (I never met one) that what went on was under the direct supervision of heaven.

A couple came to see me in my office. They had met through a bureau and were embarrassed about it. Did I disapprove? They were apprehensive and they sat primly and waited on my answer.

They brought back my youth, for that was how my elders met. In the pre-war world, love was not something that happened, it was something that you earned by your loyalty through the years. It could not be the beginning of a relationship – that was to confuse it with something trivial like being 'in love' – it was the end, the prize, the summit. I told them I would and could help them and they smiled uncertainly. I would chaperone them to a teashop, I said, if there was still a pastry in it for me!

From *Blue Heaven*, (Hodder & Stoughton Ltd).

Cleo Laine

'Ne'er change a clout till May is out' is what my Mum believed. But not me. When the first sunshine broke through after the long grey winter, I'd throw off my black wool stockings, heavy shoes and thick woolly jumper, and dress in white ankle socks, find the prettiest dress and put a ribbon in my bushy hair. I'd creep out of the house and off down the road, chirping like the birds of spring – of course, showing off when I arrived at school in all my bright finery.

It was not to last long. Mother, finding the discarded winter wear, would pack it all up and arrive at the school insisting that I be taken out of the class to be put back into the winter clothes. Oh! how embarrassed I felt. It didn't matter to me that I had a dreadful cold or a weak chest, and all the good reasons for her doing such a horrible thing. Not loving school anyway, at any time, that day I hated it and wanted to hide for ever. I also sulked for a week at home. She really could have let me have my spring day!

Nigel Hawthorne

When I was in Poland I was taken to a notorious Nazi concentration camp by a group of students. We had just

44

left the showers and had gone into an ante-room. There it was explained to me that when the guards were satisfied that the showers were full, the poisonous gas would be fed into the pipes. They indicated an aperture in the wall through which the guard would look. As I looked through it myself a small party of school children was being led through the showers by a guide. They looked in alarm as they saw they were being observed from above.

I couldn't help feeling that this must have been similar to experiences which occurred daily during those appalling years.

Christina Foyle

Reading has always been my greatest pleasure, so being a Bookseller's daughter was good fortune for me.

When I was about twelve, my father gave me a wonderful treat – a day that stays in my memory always.

He had arranged a series of literary lectures on Wednesday evenings, in the Bookshop, and Compton McKenzie was to be the speaker.

Compton McKenzie was coming over from the island of Jethou, where he lived, and my father said I could meet him at the station and dine with them both.

I was thrilled. I went off to Waterloo and waited for the train. When it arrived, there was no mistaking Compton McKenzie. Romantically good-looking – dressed in a kilt – he was one of the most attractive men I have ever met.

We took a taxi, to join my father at Kettners and then he regaled us with marvellous stories of the literary life in Soho. Just two doors away, had lived De Quincy who, with his friend Coleridge, was already sunk in the abyss of the opium addict. Round the corner in Frith Street was Hazlitt's house – and it is there that he wrote his delightful essays.

Further along Greek Street were the famous gaming rooms of Mrs Cornelys, and opposite, the Theatre Girls Club founded by Fay Compton, Compton McKenzie's sister.

In Kettners, the very restaurant where we were dining, Oscar Wilde entertained Lord Alfred Douglas and his respectable friends. The others he took to The Crown in Charing Cross Road.

We strolled back to Foyles and Compton McKenzie gave a magical talk on the best-loved novelists from Trollope to Galsworthy.

For me, a child, it was an evening of enchantment, brought back vividly to life, more than sixty years later, as I receive the latest volume of the Dictionary of National Biography, for which I had the great honour to be asked to write Compton McKenzie's biography.

Roy Hudd

Once, when I was away from home doing a summer season in Torquay, my son Max started his prayers with: 'Our Father, which art in Devon'.

Libby Purves

When I was just four years old, my father (a diplomat) was posted to Bangkok. The rest of the family travelled out to Thailand on a ship to join him. On the first night at sea, my brother, who was (and is) twenty months older than me, managed to persuade me that if I threw all my dolls out of the porthole, they would swim to Bangkok and the exercise would do them good. So I did. I suppose my mother tried to break it to me gently during the weeks of the journey that the dolls might not make it; I can't remember much. But I do remember lingering, dragging my feet on the hot dockside at the other end, glancing backwards in the hope of seeing tiny sawdust and china arms doggedly paddling towards me . . .

Oddly enough, I never blamed my brother. But from that day to this I haven't had much of an opinion of dolls. Fickle, spineless creatures.

Sir Harry Secombe, CBE

The Kindly Conspiracy

It was one of those warm hazy summer mornings that only occur in childhood. Kenny Thomas and I sat on his

mother's back doorstep looking out at the Swansea Docks across the wild triangle of blackcurrant bushes and runner bean sticks that represented the Probert's garden, contemplating on how to spend the day.

The council house back gardens stretched down the hill before us in a patchwork revelation of individual horticultural prowess. The sunflowers in the Williams's family plot which reached proudly towards their bedroom windows were the result of an accidentally spilled packet of seeds, whilst at number 7, Leger Crescent the Denton's petunias and peonies grew in the disciplined rows which ex-Sgt Major Denton, (Welsh Guards) ordained for them from the moment he had made his choice from Carter's mail order catalogue.

Cats prowled the wilderness of his next door neighbours, the Llewellyn's backyard, like miniature tigers on some Indian game reserve, occasionally making forays into the drilled plantations of the ex-Army gardener who stood constant watch over his well-ordered domain from his bedroom window, permanently perched on a spring mattress howdah, a Daisy air rifle across his withered shanks. His only victim in the past three months had been a large ginger tom cat who seemed to belong to no one in particular. He had shot it in the act of copulation with a half-Persian from the Vicarage. It was on record that the recipient of the pellet paused only briefly before finishing what it had begun and that it limped away into the shelter of the Llewellyn's scabrous weeds with a backward glance of fine disdain towards his assailant's window. This brought a spatter of applause from other bedroom window occupants who were glad to have a diversion from watching St Thomas's first eleven being annihilated by a scratch side from the Seamen's Mission on the 65-degree slope cricket pitch which bordered the gardens.

Today, though, all was quiet on the agricultural front, and only the desultory siren of a banana boat disturbed the calm of the pristine day.

'Hless go for a hwalk up to the rezzer on Hilvey Hill,' said my companion. This I immediately interpreted as 'Let's go for a walk up to the reservoir on Kilvey Hill'. Kenny had been born with a cleft palate which made his speech difficult for other people to understand. As his constant friend from the age of three I was the only one who could make out what he was saying. Even his parents had trouble. Whenever he was sent on a shopping errand by his mother I always had to go with him so that I could surreptitiously explain what he wanted. It was customary for him to make his order to the shopkeeper who would watch my lips while pretending to listen to Kenny. A kindly conspiracy in which all the local tradespeople shared.

'It's too hot to walk up the hill,' I said, my eyes on Jessie Probert who had emerged from her back door wearing her mother's tablecloth as a sarong. She was topless, but at ten years of age that was of no consequence. Jessie swayed up to the wire separating the two gardens and undulated her hips suggestively.

'I seen Dorothy Lamour last night in *Hurricane*,' she said. 'Let's play sailors and natives.'

'No thanks,' we said in unison. Jessie was a potential source of trouble – always wanting to play games which invariably ended in 'I'll show you mine if you'll show me yours.'

She stuck out her tongue and swayed off towards the Williams's fence where the head of Tom Williams was

50

just visible amongst the sunflowers. He was two years older than we were and had more to show for it.

Kenny and I breathed a collective sigh of relief and settled back on the step. I narrowed my eyes deliberately and pretended that I was in Africa. *Trader Horn* had played our local flea pit three months before and we were both hooked on the African jungle. The bean sticks and blackcurrant bushes looked like dense forest if one had enough imagination and God knows I had plenty. I caught the swish of a tail in the undergrowth and I was off on the trail of a lion.

'Try squinting up your eyes and pretending the Probert's garden's like a jungle,' I said to Kenny. 'Look at the lion hiding up in the bush waiting to make the kill.' I pointed to the cat's tail waving amongst the leaves next door.

'Oh yeagh.' Kenny peered uncertainly in a different direction.

'Come on, you two,' said Mrs Thomas behind us. 'Go and get some meat from the butcher's.' She was a little plump woman who always smelt of apples and the sly hint of gin. By nature a pleasant person, she was however given to fits of sudden rage, the legacy of having for a husband a docker whose meal timetable did not always coincide with opening hours.

We stood up reluctantly. Kenny, in search of my imaginary lion's tail, had spotted something far more interesting and just as primeval in the antics of Jessie Probert and Tom Williams dimly seen through the screen of sunflowers and blackcurrants.

'I want a quarter of a pound of steak and a half a pound of sausages,' said Mrs Thomas. 'On the book,' she added quickly.

We repeated the order together.

'That's right, good boys.' She looked at me with her eyebrows raised and I nodded slightly to let her know that I had the message right. 'Here's a penny each for going.'

This was an unexpected bonus and we clutched the coins gleefully as she took them from her apron pocket and placed them in our outstretched palms.

We made a bee-line across the Patch to Mrs Morris's, a widow who kept a sweet shop in the front parlour of her council house. It was illegal, but the rent man turned a blind eye to the fact out of compassion and a sweet tooth. The choice was agonizing. For a penny we could have a quarter of Sharp's toffees or a lucky packet, which usually contained a liquorice root, transfers to stick on the back of your hand, some tiger nuts, a couple of sweet cigarettes and sherbet suckers. There were also pear drops, gob stoppers which changed colour as you sucked them, and an assortment of chocolate bars.

Eventually after much consultation while Mrs Morris, in a cross-over pinny and carpet slippers, waited patiently for our decision I settled for a lucky packet and Kenny pointed to the glass jar of pear drops. She handed me my purchase and, making a cone from a torn piece of the *South Wales Evening Post*, she dropped in it a half dozen of the pink and white sweets, hesitated half a second, looked at Kenny's upturned face, and added another two. Our pennies were duly passed over and, the complicated transaction completed, she put them into a little tin cash box on the mantelpiece. I thanked her on behalf of myself and my friend, who was incapable of doing so himself, having further complicated his speech defect with a mouthful of pear drops.

Outside in the street I examined my lucky packet. Beside the usual contents there was a small green tin frog which made a clicking noise when a tab of metal

52

underneath it was pressed, and a strange looking object which appeared to be a twig. I put the transfers in my pocket for later use – I needed a saucer of water and infinite patience to get a perfect picture on the back of my hand. I would also get the back of my father's hand if he found me doing it. The sherbet sweets I disposed of by putting them in my mouth, and clicking the frog in rhythm with my chewing we sauntered contentedly down St Leger Crescent.

By the time we had got as far as Mrs Evans the Pop, a lady who sold flagons of a home-made brew without which no Sunday dinner was complete, and which had a tendency to explode if kept too long, Kenny was on the last of his pear drops and was trying to make it last as long as possible by taking it out of his mouth and licking it between his fingers. I was down to the twig which I was loth to try, but I had been brought up not to waste anything. I stopped by Mrs Evans's gate and licked it tentatively. It had a funny bitter-sweet taste which I had never before encountered. I closed my eyes and chewed a small piece, rolling it around on the tongue in the true tradition of the connoisseur. When I opened my eyes again, still unable to identify the taste, I found myself being observed through the dusty privet hedge. The ginger tom cat which belonged to no one lay in the shade watching me with slitted amber eyes, tail swishing. I backed away nervously. In my daydreams I would fearlessly stalk the African jungle in search of dangerous game, but in real life I had a great respect for all animals, having been kicked by a cow in Cardigan on holiday.

I stretched out my hand towards it in a protective gesture. It was the hand that held the twig, and the battered head came forward to sniff it. The smell seemed to please the cat and it took the twig in its mouth.

'Hless go,' said Kenny nervously. We were both aware of the animal's reputation for wildness and the two intrepid African explorers beat a hasty retreat.

We slowed up as we got to the bottom of the street, looked at each other and began laughing.

'Bang. Bang!' I shouted, clicking my tin frog. 'Fancy being afraid of a cat.'

'Yeagh,' smiled Kenny, his lips pink.

'You look like a girl with lipstick on,' I said. I made him look in the window of the Co-op. We fell about laughing again.

It was when we got to the ironmonger's that I had the feeling that I was being followed. I turned around and there behind me was the ginger tom cat. Its face bore as near an expression of bliss as it could muster and it wrapped itself around my legs, purring and licking its lips. In cat terms this was tantamount to the conversion of St Paul on the road to Damascus. But this was Port Tennant Road and led to Neath and I had not been aware of any blinding light. Then it dawned on Kenny and me that it must have been the twig from the lucky packet. To this day I have no idea what it was, but the effect on the cat was incredible. I could not shake it off and it walked alongside me all the way to the butcher's. When Kenny tried to smooth it, its claws came out and it growled a warning, but I could have kicked it up the street and it would have come back for more. I know, I tried it.

The butcher's shop was next door but one to an undertaker's and my mother never became a customer there for that reason. 'It's not nice,' she would say. The legend 'Family Butcher' in raised white letters on the window coupled with its proximity to the funeral parlour used to put bizarre thoughts in my mind. I imagined rows of families, neatly butchered, hanging on hooks in the refrigerator, and the pig's head on display in the window with a tomato in its mouth looked too much like the late Mr Howells for comfort.

We went into the shop together, the three of us, the cat firmly wedging itself between my legs. Before we could give our order in unison, the butcher's large wife, who sat by the cash register, shouted, 'Get that cat out of here.' Her husband, in a straw hat and striped apron, nodded in agreement and sharpened his knife a little faster.

'It won't leave us,' I said.

'He's not serving you with that thing in here.'

Her husband nodded again.

I was in a terrible dilemma. Unless I was there to translate the order, Kenny might finish up with anything, and at the same time we would never get served if I stayed in the shop because the cat would not leave without me.

Meanwhile, Kenny, who had never been aware of the fact that I was the one who really did the messages for his mother, could not understand what I was getting excited about.

'Htake hthe hcat outhide,' he said calmly. 'HI'll hget hthe horder.'

'Get that bloody cat out.' The butcher's wife was getting hysterical.

I picked the cat up and left the shop with a heavy heart. They wouldn't even let me stand in the doorway and I stood out of sight in the undertaker's doorway with the cat kneading my chest with its claws through my short-sleeved celanese shirt.

Kenny came out a few minutes later.

'What did you get?' I said anxiously.

55

'Hsteak hand hsauhage.' He was beginning to think I was going potty.

I breathed a sigh of relief which ruffled the fur on the cat's face and sent it into fresh ecstacy.

'Oh, gerroff,' I detached its claws from my shirt and threw the cat roughly to the ground.

We got back to Kenny's mother's just as the church clock struck half past twelve. She was on her way up the stairs as we came in through the kitchen door followed by the ginger tom. Kenny proudly handed over the newspaper-wrapped parcel.

'There's good boys,' she said.

I stood waiting anxiously as she unfolded the bundle. I knew that Kenny had ordered steak and sausages and a cautious feel had confirmed that he had got what he had asked for. The important question was the amount he had ordered. The difference between ordering a quarter of a pound of steak and a half a pound of sausages, and a *half* a pound of steak and a quarter of a pound of sausages could upset the family budget for a week.

Mrs Thomas's smile faded as she saw what we had bought. One of her sudden rages shook her and before she spoke I knew that my suspicions had been confirmed.

'Half a pound of steak!' she screamed, weighing it physically in her hand, and mentally in her mind against the half bottle of gin the extra quarter of a pound represented. 'Who do you think I am, Mrs Rothschild?' As she delivered this line, she hurled the steak from her in a fine theatrical gesture. Kenny ducked, I swerved, and it hit the rent man, who had just appeared in the doorway, in the chest.

It fell to the floor and we all stood still like a waxwork tableau. All, that is, except the ginger tom who, with that lightning change of mood to which all cats are prone, transferred its affection from me to the steak and in a blur of movement seized it in its jaws and streaked through the rent man's legs into the garden.

Three seconds later ex-RSM Denton's air rifle cracked, and the despairing cry 'Missed the bastard!' revealed the route the cat had taken.

Both the rent man and myself found ourselves in a brief tangle in the doorway and I ran home to lunch. We had fish and chips. I don't know what the Thomas's had because it was some time before I could bring myself to ask and by that time Kenny had forgotten.

Many years later, when he and I had gone our separate ways, my mother was standing at a bus stop reading the *Swansea Evening Post*'s first report on the part played by the town's territorial artillery regiment, to which I belonged, in the North African landings.

Somebody touched her sleeve. It was Kenny Thomas, and his eyes were bright with tears. 'He's gone to Africa without me after all,' he said and walked away.

From *Goon for Lunch* (Michael Joseph Ltd).

Peter Barkworth

The first time

'Oh I do want to be an actor when I grow up,' I said to my mother when we got home. I don't remember saying

57

it, but she never forgot it and would remind me of it from time to time.

I had been in a play called *Simple Simon*, put on by the 2nd Kenton Wolf-cub pack in our hall next door to the Methodist church at the bottom of the road. It had been written and produced by our leader, Akela, a small, dumpy woman with a brown face which had a lot of wrinkles in it. She had a quiet voice and smiled a lot, which accounted for the wrinkles round her eyes.

It was just after my fifth birthday and it was my first part in any play. I was Simple Simon, and I wore a white apron over my wolf-cub's uniform, and on my head, instead of my cap with its green segments separated by gold braid, I had a tall white hat with a wider bit at the top, like a chef's.

Of the play itself I can remember nothing; but if I plunge my thoughts back to that winter evening in 1934 I can still recall with the utmost vividness the sheer sensual pleasure I felt from being on a stage. The lights were shining into my eyes and on to my face. The people in the audience were out there somewhere but I couldn't see them because they weren't lit and I was: they were in the darkness and I was in the light. It was my first sight of that great black hole which the auditorium becomes during a performance, and it made me feel powerful and alone. I could sense there were a lot of people there, though, for my voice sounded different: instead of ringing round the hard, bare walls as it had at the rehearsals it was muffled now, absorbed in all the people and their heavy winter clothes. Apparently there wasn't a seat to be had, and some had to stand at the back. I could hear vague audience noises: the rustling of dresses, the creaking of chairs, the occasional nose-blow and cough.

The little play, which was part of a longer evening's

58

entertainment, went as planned and there were no mishaps. The audience was attentive and laughed a bit from time to time. But what was best was the clapping at the end, which got louder as the curtains were opened and quieter every time they closed. Bowing was nice; but even nicer were all the congratulations afterwards. My father put a hand on my shoulder and said, 'Well done, laddie', and my mother said, 'Very good, Peter', and pride shone from her pretty face. Their approbation mattered much more than anybody else's and so it was to continue through my professional life. Part of me always did it for them; and when they died something at the back of me, some safety, some solidity had gone: there seemed less reason for doing it, a diminished purpose . . . and so it continues today.

But then, in 1934, when I had my first taste of their approval, it was glorious. I was completely and utterly happy. There could be no pleasure like it. No wonder I wanted to be an actor when I grew up.

Extract from *First Houses* by Peter Barkworth, reprinted by kind permission of Secker and Warburg Ltd.

Angela Rumbold, CBE

Member of Parliament

When I was about ten a friend and I decided that we were going to embark upon the project of holding a dog show. For two little girls who were around the ages of nine and ten this was quite an enterprise.

My father was full of admiration for the way in which we booked the field and set up the prizes and the whole course for dogs to be shown and for the entries to be judged. This was, perhaps, my very first endeavour to set up and organize a show for public entertainment. Doubtless, it was a fore-runner of things to come, but I think it was something that my father always took as being an indication that his small daughter and her friend had nothing if not the spirit of 'nothing ventured, nothing gained'.

The dog that won the prize was a very large shaggy sheepdog. We were delighted with his success but not quite so delighted when he attacked all of the rather carefully made prize rosettes that we had cobbled together with difficulty, since in those days there were still clothing coupons and, therefore, it was not so easy to get ribbons.

The afternoon was a great success and we had a number of letters from quite eminent people, since all of this took place on a football field belonging to one of the Cambridge Colleges. We had some extremely interesting and distinguished entrants to our little dog show.

Naomi James

My memories of school days are blurred, partly because I was a lazy little girl who always attempted to get out of working by smiling a lot (it was not a satisfactory ploy) and partly because I have an appalling memory anyway. Surprisingly, therefore, the one recollection that springs to mind concerns the time *before* I went to school.

According to my mother I anticipated my entrance into the big wide world with a mixture of excitement and dread – we lived in a remote place in the country (in New Zealand) and hardly saw a soul outside the family. We four children were shy for that reason and my two sisters already at school had told me enough to fill me with misgivings.

They were delivered every morning by tractor to the shelter of a large oak tree along a quiet country road, there to await the schoolbus. (By the time I went we had a bus shelter down the end of our road – a mere one mile walk.) There was no television then, only books and radio, but I possessed a fertile visual imagination which furnished me with graphic images of classrooms and teachers and the wonderful things that went on there – as unrealistic as any four year old could think up. The only part of the school I'd actually seen was the door of the small school house, in front of which was a landing with steps leading up to it.

In my mind's eye I often viewed that landing until, one day, I came by a wonderful piece of information. I was told that every child was given milk to drink at school. We lived on a dairy farm so milk should have been no novelty, but I detected an important difference: this was *bottled* milk. We only drank cows' milk straight from the tank and sometimes it was still warm. After sufficient for ourselves and the cats was removed from the tank the rest was turned into cream and pale yellow whey which was left to curdle and then fed to the pigs.

But school milk was going to be *real* bottled milk, brought to the school in a truck. The trouble was, I had never seen a milk bottle, but I had seen a beer bottle. And often, after the beer had been drunk, my mother would refill the empty bottles with home-made ginger beer. So obviously, they could be used for milk too. From then on, in my musing, a row of stately brown beer bottles of milk would appear on the landing beside the door and every morning, as the children tripped into school, they would each take one, pop open the top with their teeth and swill the milk down.

Throughout my first day at school images shattered all around me, but none, strangely enough, left any lasting impression – except the travesty of the milk. The sight of a small white half-pint bottle with a tinsel top and a straw sticking out of it and tasting of tank milk was a sad blow to my feelings from which I have never quite recovered. My imagination has continued to serve me up wonderful dreams and images but on that day I became a realist.

Tony Hart

In 1934 I was, arguably, fortunate enough to be accepted into a resident Choir School in the West End of London. It so happened that I joined the choir just two weeks before the end of the Christmas term. Such a very small boy, I had little idea of the length of a school term and

thoroughly enjoyed the lead up to Christmas with its attendant parties, pantomimes and carols. All culminating in sausage and mash, a bran tub with presents and the Midnight Mass. I had never been up so late and never heard anything so exciting as Gounod's Saint Cecilia with a full choir. The next morning I travelled home with my older cousin who was four years ahead of me. Full of enthusiasm for my new boarding school I was actually looking forward to going back. In the taxi from Victoria my cousin told me that it would be three months before the Easter holidays, no pantomimes and that there could be only one visit by a parent during the term. No wonder my heart still misses a beat when I'm near Broadcasting House and see Butterfield's sooty spire emerging from the Rag Trade that still surrounds it!

Floella Benjamin

Surprise, surprise

I loved my schooldays but there were one or two surprises waiting for me when I came to England and started school here. It was quite different from Trinidad. I remember my first day at primary school, the other kids invited me to play tag and although I was a very fast runner I was eventually cornered by a boy called Norman who proceeded to kiss me! I was so shocked I let fly and gave him a couple of good hard slaps. Well, how was I to know it was kiss chase they were playing! Norman was the school heart throb so I was sent to Coventry for beating him up!

But the biggest surprise to me was racism. In Trinidad no one called me names because of my colour, so I was very upset when it happened at school in England. One incident I remember was on the rounders field: I kept whacking the ball into orbit, much to the annoyance of one girl called Dorothy and her small gang of trouble-makers. Dorothy and her followers started insulting me and calling me racist names. Now, not exactly being the shy retiring type, I eventually decided I'd had enough from Dorothy and her friends. So wielding my rounders bat I lined them up against a wall and one by one forced the cowering girls to apologize and promise never to call me names again. They never did, at least not to my face.

This is just one of the many times I reacted against the racist jibes I had to face at school. Strangely enough Dorothy wrote to me the other day telling me how much she and her children loved watching me on the television. School can be a tough and cruel place but I always remember what my mum said every morning to all six of her children: 'Education is your passport to success.' How right she was.

Rachel Billington

Young love

It was the most thrilling moment of my eight years. A pony had arrived for me. A horse-box had brought her in the afternoon from my aunt's farm. She was called Swallow and, like a swallow, she was black with flashes of white. Since it was winter her coat was thick and furry and when I threw my arms round her it was like hugging a toy bear. Yet she was warm, breathing out white air through her nostrils, moving her feet, turning her head round to push at me. The love I felt for her was the pent-up emotion of years of yearning. At last I had a pony and I loved her more than I loved myself.

Darkness came early that November day; there was wind, rain. I lay in my snug bed and thought of Swallow out in our little paddock. She was alone, without her friends from the farm: she was in a strange place. My imagination pictured her desolation. The noise of the wind turned into a lonely whinnying. I knew just how she must be feeling and became more and more miserable. Sleep was impossible.

Around midnight when our house was dark and quiet, I crept downstairs, found my wellington boots and went outside. To my surprise, the night was utterly peaceful, the wild wind gone and with it the wild whinnying. Above my head there was a glorious array of stars, making it quite easy for me to find my way through the garden to the paddock. I saw Swallow at once, a large black blob in the middle of the field. I had expected signs of terrible unhappiness. What I saw was a fat contented pony nibbling grass under a starlit sky. It took her a few seconds even to raise her head and then she only gave me an incurious glance.

In a flash I understood that this pony was quite separate from me. My huge love could not cross the divide between animal and human. Whatever I strove to make her, she would remain herself, a jolly little pony and I would remain myself, a pony-mad little girl. Turning from this realization, I ran back to the house, flung off my boots and jumped into my bed. Where I slept soundly till morning.

© Copyright Rachel Billington.

Bruce Kent

Chairman, Campaign for Nuclear Disarmament

When I committed adultery, aged eight

It was the mole that caused all the trouble and led me into Sin. There were a lot of moles in the grounds of our prep. school and they made a mess of the lawn, to the fury of the gardener. So he set traps. As a result one afternoon I found a nice fat mole lying dead on the grass where he had left it.

Was it a Lady mole or a Gentleman mole I wondered since it had dawned on me that there were differences.

So I examined the mole in the greatest detail and with very guilty feelings. In my bones I knew that nice boys did not do this sort of thing. I forget the result of the inspection, but I do know that my conscience began to work overtime. It was quite clear in our prayer books *'Thou shalt not commit adultery'*. This adultery, which no one would talk about and which the RI teacher skated over, must include the unauthorized personal examination of the private parts of moles. It was also made clear that this Adultery was a Mortal Sin.

Only after I had refused communion for weeks on end, on account of my Sin, was it explained to me that the Sixth Commandment did not cover moles. But I still wasn't told what it did cover.

Barbara Cartland

Pershore, Worcestershire 1907

I am walking along a country road holding on to the perambulator which my Nanny is pushing. Inside it is my new baby brother Ronald who was born in January.

I am very bored with having him with us and have already said to my mother:

'Mummy do let us send that baby away. Everyone asks after him and no-one asks after me!'

I think the real reason I resent him is that my mother looks at him in a different way from how she looks at me. Her eyes seem to have a light behind them and her voice is full of love.

I know now I am not part of her as I was before, but

complete in myself, and I feel alone. Even when people are all round me I am alone and it's a strange and rather frightening feeling.

We reach a cottage where Nanny is to leave some soup for a woman who is ill. While she talks at the door I cross the road.

There is a gate into the park which is open.

I stand beside it and look at the crimson poppies among the grasses, the purple cuckoo-flowers, the white and gold marguerites, and the blue love-in-the-mist.

Suddenly as I am looking at them the flowers seem to come nearer to me, to get larger and larger.

There is a strange vibration coming from them and I think that I can see them growing, living, breathing . . .

It is so extraordinary and so exciting that I stand staring at the flowers and I know they are alive as I am.

'Barbara!' It is my Nanny's voice. 'What are you doing? Come here at once, you naughty little girl!'

The spell is broken, I run back across the road . . .

1910

I know there are goblins with huge heads and little bodies burrowing beneath the hills.

There are nymphs soft as the mist in the silver lakes and streams; huge green dragons, fighting and breathing fire, lurk in the darkness of the pine woods.

There are two big trees very close together in the secret part of the garden, and when I am going to sleep I know that if I can squeeze between them I shall find all that I am seeking, although I am not certain what it is.

Sometimes I have a glimpse of a fairy amongst the flowers – I see her out of the corner of my eye, but when I turn my head she has gone.

The fairies dance on the lawn at night and leave a circle of mushrooms; so I know they have been there.

In the winter when the leafless branches of the trees are silhouetted against the sunset I have a strange feeling within me as if they lift me up into the sky.

1912
I have read *Alice Through the Looking-Glass* and I know now that what I have been trying to do before I go to sleep is to step through the Looking-Glass.

That is the world that fascinates and draws me, the world I sense between the trees, the world of the goblins and fairies, a world behind the world.

I know it is very near me, a shadow behind my head, just round the corner, at the top of the stairs.

I am determined to find it.

Sometimes when I am alone in the garden I put my ear against the trunk of a tree. I can hear it breathing and living. Everything has life in it like the life in me.

But there is another part of life which I cannot hear or touch, yet it is there through the Looking-Glass.

Dr John Habgood
Archbishop of York

My first public appearance was as an elf in a dancing display. I wore a green floppy costume with diamond-shaped points hanging down round my waist and a green balaclava helmet with floppy ears. I must have been three or four at the time, on the podgy side, extremely solemn and distinctly un-elf-like.

A group of us were supposed to dance the polka, but having emerged onto the stage I stood in the centre of it staring at the audience, fascinated, not budging an inch.

'Dance John, dance' whispered the frantic dancing mistress, loud enough for everybody in the room to hear. I gave a single hop. The audience roared. 'Dance John, dance.' More audience reaction.

Meanwhile all the genuine elves polka-ing vigorously round the stage were being totally ignored. By the time they had finished I had managed a third hop and received a standing ovation.

It just goes to show how unfair life can be.

Lord Brabourne

When I was at school, we had a Matron (or a 'Dame' as she was called at this particular school) who I did not get on with at all well. She used to do a great deal of knitting and one day, after we had had a disagreement, she left out on a table a large skein of knitting wool which she was rolling into a ball. When she was out of the room, I noticed a pot of Radio Malt (a treacly 'strengthening' medicine which pours rather like glue and which is now rather out of fashion) and I poured this treacly substance on to the wool. When the poor lady came back, she found the most appalling (and from my point of view satisfactory) mess! As can be imagined, I was extremely unpopular for a considerable time after this successful venture!

Lynsey de Paul

I have an elder brother who often had his friends around to play in the garden. On one such occasion, he was eight and I was four, he and his friends decided to behave like little boys and so they all lined up against the garden wall and with perfect arched projectorate, peed up against it. Always having been somewhat of a tomboy, I thought this looked jolly good fun and decided to join in. To my confusion and horror it did not quite work out the same and I soaked my little grey dress. Amidst howls of disappointment, my mother gave me my first introduction on the differences between the sexes and my brother was severely reprimanded for gross misbehaviour in the garden.

The second anecdote was also when I was four years old. I was always much littler than the other girls but rather fast at running. One day we had a race in school and I did not realize that I had won because I had run under the finishing tape, and was belting down another playground before I was hailed back.

Mary Whitehouse

I long ago came to the conclusion that I wasn't really a very nice child! I used to get on my bicycle and take myself off into the Cheshire lanes – complete with hunks of Cheshire cheese and bottles of pop – so that I wouldn't have to help my poor Mum with all the washing up and the 'mangling' – an activity unheard of now – of the family washing.

Why do I say 'my poor Mum'? Because she had four children under six, the eldest of whom was very severely handicapped with polio. Mind you, my sister was full of life and up to all manner of tricks herself. She would get me to put her on my bike, give her a push to start her off, then she would pedal with her 'good leg' and swing her stiff calipered 'bad' one back and forwards to knock the other pedal round. And I had to stand in the road and wait for her to come back!

But I wasn't always so accommodating. In order to take her to town I had to push her bathchair up a long steep railway bridge – and I was stretched out almost horizontal in the effort – but when I got to the top I would let her go and she, frantically, would steer, hopefully, amongst the legs of panic-stricken passers by. As I said I was not a very nice child. But it's nice to recall now what good friends my sister and I became and still are!

Larry Adler

The odd thing about this childhood memory is that while I'm sure it's true I'm equally sure it can't be.

I was about five and on holiday with my parents at Betterton, Maryland. We were on the beach and I went wading. At one point the ground fell away and I dropped a fair distance and found myself under water. I wasn't frightened – this is the first improbability – and there was a fine golden glow from the sun. I walked around quite happily, found the place where I'd gone under, climbed back up and went back to the beach. My mother was crying hysterically, she was sure I'd drowned, and a life-guard was at that moment searching for me.

First, I couldn't swim. Second, I was always scared and still am if my head goes under water at any time. Yet the memory is perhaps the strongest of my childhood.

For baksheesh here's a joke based on the same subject. A Jewish grandmother, on the beach, watches her grandson wading. He suddenly goes under, the grandmother screams, a life-guard goes out, can't find the kid. He gets another guard, they row out, dive down, can't find the kid. They radio for a helicopter, it circles over the water and, in the depths, they see the body floating. The kid is fished out, brought to the beach, given artificial respiration, kiss of life, and after several minutes his limbs stir and he gasps for breath.

'He's alive,' shouts a guard, 'we've saved him!'

Says the grandmother, 'He had a *hat*!'

Russ Abbot

I have always attributed my love of nice clothes to the fact that as the youngest of five brothers I always wandered around looking like Compo whilst my eldest brother looked like Anthony Andrews – by the time his clothes reached me via the other three, Steptoe wouldn't have given them yard room! Needless to say that in this male dominated household my dear mother never won the battle of the loo seat!

I remember one incident vividly or should I say painfully. My father always kept his golf clubs in the garage and it was only a matter of time before one of my brothers and myself slipped into the garage to show each other how easy it was.

My brother solemnly placed the tee (heavily disguised as an egg cup from the kitchen) on the ground proclaiming that the idea was not to move the tee at all. We would both learn differently a lot later on in life. I decided to take a closer look at all this and lay down on the ground full length to get the full benefit of my brother's obvious superiority in this sport. He swung his club and I woke up on the floor of the kitchen not knowing which was bigger, the lump on my forehead where he had hit me or the ice pack that was on it! My brother had used my head as the biggest ball he could find!

Moral: never play golf in the garage with egg cups and at all times stand well clear!!

Leo Abse

Member of Parliament

I remember well the details of that fateful day although I was only six years five months old. With my eight-year-old brother Wilfred, I had, for reasons then obscure to me, been dispatched to another part of the city to stay with my maternal grandparents. This was more than acceptable to me since I was the favourite of my grandfather, a Talmudist who, I claim, was the first man to speak Welsh with a Yiddish accent: it was less congenial to my brother but, since he was the favourite of my paternal grandmother, a German born belligerent atheist, a woman of the Enlightenment, who lived but a few hundred yards away from the Talmudist, Wilfred was not over-fretful. The excursion would give both of us a full opportunity to play off the grandparents who, until their deaths, competed with each other for the grandchildren: we never failed to exploit the splendid opportunities that gave ever increasing pocket money as the grandfather and grandmother over-trumped each other.

After a few days sojourn we were told we could return home and that we would find there a splendid present, a new baby brother, who, my grandfather told me, would be called Daniel and who, my grandmother, ever resenting the Biblical resonances, told me would be called

Dannie. Well augmented with ninepence from the respective grandparents, we commenced our long walk home. I doubt if we aware of the tale of the Magi and we certainly were not guided by any stars on our journey; but we decided after much discussion that we must arrive with a gift. We quickly reached agreement as to the nature of our presentation; no silly gewgaw for us. What the new brother must have was reading material, for in Wales, unlike England, the term intellectual is not pejorative and we were brought up, too, in a Jewish ethos which taught us that in the beginning was the Word. But Wilfred and I fell out as to what reading material was suitable.

I wanted to take him, for instruction on the wider world, *The Children's Newspaper*, an Arthur Mee publication, of which, as became a future politician, I was an avid reader; but Wilfred thought a coloured comic was more suitable, a choice which doubtless the future Emeritus Professor of psychiatry anticipated would stimulate the imagination of the child. In the end, with our pocket money, we bought both. When my turn came to enter my brother's bedroom and I saw the sleeping babe I became afflicted with doubt about his capacity to appreciate my gift; but my mother reassured me and told me that Dannie would enjoy it when he was awake. Now I think my mother deceived me and my present was not passed on. But Wilfred's comic, full of fantasy, larks and fun was evidently given to him. How else can we explain that Dannie is the President of Britain's Poetry Society?

The Rt. Hon. Jeremy Thorpe

As a result of my father being on the German's Black List, I spent the first three years of the War at school in the United States. When America came into the War the school decided that in order to release manpower for the fighting forces, domestic chores should be taken over by the students.

I volunteered enthusiastically to look after the pigs and regarded myself as highly privileged to have my request granted. Shortly after this, my American Aunt, who was as kind as she was large, came down to see me and insisted on being involved as far as possible in the activities of the school.

Since it was winter I used to take a large bucket of hot steaming garbage through the snow on the sledge – to the pigs – fortunately it was all down hill from the school to the pig sty. My long-suffering Aunt readily assented to the suggestion that she should travel down with me and duly decked out in mink coat and fur boots she took up her place on the sledge. In retrospect I suppose her added weight accelerated the speed at which we were to travel. We set off at a cracking pace and to my horror hit a tree stump that was carefully camouflaged by the snow. The Aunt, sledge and pig food ended up in a heap and from then on I determined that feeding the pigs was a job for one man and passengers were to be avoided!

Sir Geoffrey Chandler, CBE

Guilt and cowardice

My elder sister, thirteen, said she was stronger minded than I. I, two years younger, disputed this.

'Shut the door,' she said, as I left her bedroom.

'Say please,' said I.

'You *will* shut the door because I am stronger minded than you.'

'I will shut the door if you say please.'

'We'll see,' said she.

Time passed. I shut the door.

I did so, I told her, because I was better natured than her.

We designed orange skin teeth for our visit to the dentist. The technique is simple. Cut from the peel of an orange a piece the shape of a gumshield; incise a line laterally, stopping short of each end; make short vertical cuts across this line and place under the lips, pith side outwards; protrude the tongue. For a more dramatic effect one of the resulting teeth can be excised.

Giggling hard we arrived at the dentist's door. My courage failed. I took my teeth out. My sister smiled graciously at the attendant who opened the door, combining this with a look of contempt at me, took her place in the dentist's chair and exposed her dentures to his interested gaze.

She would not make orange skin teeth with me again.

I blushed easily. 'Who didn't shut the summerhouse window?' asked my father. 'Ah, I can see,' he observed, as my cheeks turned scarlet, though I was innocent of the offence. 'Who has been using an excess of lavatory paper?' (earth closets, if insufficient earth is used, are peculiarly revealing). My cheeks burnt with knowledge of guilt. 'Who has . . . ?' I blushed. The question could have been anything. There was no need to finish it.

We accounted for our pocket money weekly which my father regarded as a sensible educational discipline. My accounts, cobbled together after an hour poring over them on the lavatory seat, frequently did not add up. 'Can you show me,' asked my father, 'the ninepence you have over?', having observed that the original 1/4d in hand, plus a 2/- bet I had won from him over the volume of a watering can, and expenditure of miscellaneous sums totalling 3/10d equalled a deficit rather than the surplus I had indicated. I went upstairs, borrowed the sum from my more provident sister, and demonstrated the accuracy of my accounts.

The second state was worse than the first.

Envoi:

My elder sister is my closest friend. She remains stronger minded than I.

I feel guilty, though no longer blush, as I go through the green channel of the Customs.

I dislike money, feel ill over income tax forms, and am hopeless at fund-raising.

My father, a distinguished chest physician, also brought us up with a living awareness of the Hippocratic oath and the belief, as he put it, that one should try and leave the world a little better than one found it.

Jean Rook

Assistant Editor, Daily Express

This girl and I were the same age – unlucky thirteen. I was fat, and wore specs. She had ruler-flat hips, a waist she could have squeezed inside an elastic band, and a top like two cute little bouncing tennis balls.

My Mum made me wear plaits. My rival had a stunningly fashionable flip-under Page Boy hair-do.

In her bottle-green, box-pleated school gymslip she was always band-box neat. In my gaping pleats, strained by Mars Bars, I looked like a broken green bottle.

We both travelled over the Yorkshire moors, by train, to Whitby Grammar – a mixed school, though I only mixed with other dull, bashful girls. Miss Marvellous had a smashing Sixth Form boyfriend who joined the train three stops from Whitby.

And she had *her own carriage*.

Only the school's most popular people were allowed in that carriage. Bagged by my rival and her friends. Closed to everyone but her elite, sophisticated set.

I can still hear the sounds of unseen revelry from that magic carriage. And, since those were the days when you could lean out of a train window without losing your head, I can still see Wonder Girl leaning out to wave to her boyfriend.

Her profile, so much higher than mine, became etched on my mind. The long, upswept, spec-less eyelashes. The uptipped top that proved she could cope with a bra.

I ached, with all the small, but huge-hipped agonies

of youth, to look like her. I yearned to be in that charismatic carriage. I lost sleep, tossing in my mind how I could grow up, and become thinner, and glamorous, overnight, and break into her magic circle.

But every day, at 4.15, it was closed to me – and the door slammed in my spotty face.

So I started my own carriage – empty at first except for another lumpy girl with bottle-green bunches. But since we had this reputation for being amusing, it soon filled up. We even got a waiting list to join.

And I got my own boyfriend, who rode home with me, across the moors, from the station. In the glimmering dusk we would pedal in our billowing yellow plastic bicycle capes, holding wet, chapped, slippery hands.

Then I moved. And forgot that marvellous, maddening, fabulous rival girl who had tortured my youth. Or pretended to forget.

Two summers ago, and nearly 40 years on, she wrote to me. She was, she said, deprecatingly, 'an ordinary housewife – very boring.' She read everything I wrote, and had seen me on TVAM. We simply must meet up 'for old friendship sake.'

Friendship!

I didn't refuse to meet her for sweet revenge. I just couldn't have borne it if my never really forgotten, or secretly forgiven idol had grey hairs and a middle-aged spread.

She wrote back for a signed photo to prove how well she'd known me at school.

I sent her one, with a chummy message. Because I know how badly beaten you feel when someone won't let you join.

Lord Grade of Elstree

During the First World War my family moved out to Reigate, which was a lovely country town. Unlike our school in the East End of London there were only two Jewish boys in my class, myself and one other boy, and we became great rivals which eventually led to a showdown. Until this point in my life, I had never hit anyone and had never been in a fight. But now there was no avoiding the situation and I didn't want my new friends in Reigate to think me a coward, so even though I hate violence and always have, I arranged to fight my rival in Reigate Park.

I was really dreading it, but to my surprise, I discovered that I had an extremely powerful right-hand punch, and was able to give as good as I got. The fight lasted about an hour, during which time we both took a lot of punishment – though there was no clear winner. After this we both gained a degree of respect for each other, and became quite good friends. The best thing about this incident is that it gave me a certain physical confidence in myself that I'd never had before, and when a few months later, we returned to London, instead of avoiding the bully at school who'd previously been the bane of my life, I actually went looking for him. True to form, he tried to punch me in the stomach, but this time I was ready for him. With my new-found confidence, I grabbed him, pinned his arms behind his back and squeezed him until he almost cried. He never came looking for me again.

Roy Kinnear

It was Friday the 8th September 1942. I was eight years old, my sister ten. We lived in Wigan, right next door to our Aunt Gladys and Uncle John. Our father was in the RAF and our mother had gone down the weekend before to visit him at a place called Uxbridge which we were told was near London. We'd been told she'd decided to stay down for the week.

St Michael's Church Junior School was at the top of the street and Aunty Gladys gave us lunch while our mother worked in the bank.

On that Friday, we'd had our lunch, and I was playing on the carpet with a Dinky toy – a double decker bus painted light blue and yellow it was. We were about to go back to school when Aunty Gladys said that she had some bad news for us and we had to be brave. Our father was dead. My sister wept uncontrollably. I tried to cry but couldn't. How can you cry when your world has fallen apart?

Paul Eddington

About forty-five years ago – astronomers will be able to tell you the exact date – I was sitting at my desk one night doing the boarding school version of homework: 'prep'.

The sighs and scratching of pens were suddenly interrupted by the senior master. 'Leave your work', he said, 'and go straight out on to the playing fields. I'll see your teachers tomorrow and make it all right. This is something you may never see again.'

We rushed out into the night to see a near magical display of the Northern Lights, the Aurora Borealis. Great curtains of light – green, blue, purple and scarlet were sweeping across the sky. Seldom if ever has such a sight been seen so far south.

A wise man!

Tessa Sanderson, MBE

I started my javelin career by sheer accident – it was a challenge.

In school, I used to win eveything except the javelin. I had a friend called Noreen Morgan, a tall lanky girl, and of course, she was the school javelin champion. One day she challenged me to a duel. I took up the opportunity and did a few secret training practices with my school teacher, while my friend felt she did not have to practice as no one in the county had ever beaten her.

Sports Day arrived. The challenge was on – at the end of the competition I beat her!

In those days, fish and chips out of newspaper was a great attraction for a school kid and my friend had to buy them for me for one week!

So, that was how I got into javelin throwing – for a week's supply of fish and chips from my friend from a special shop!

Sarah Miles

Trees were always my comrades, next to animals, trees gave me all the comfort I needed as a litle girl and possibly this little girl never grew up. I feel that trees are the caretakers of the world, we are merely camping down for a while.

Have you ever planted a tree? You should try one day: it is very rewarding, and fun too. You can actually hear the tree saying 'Thank You! Thank You!'

My very first memory as a tiny tot is of puffy white clouds, blue sky and trees swooshing in the wind. I always had a dream of being able to sing, and since I was forbidden to sing anywhere within close proximity of the house where I lived with my brothers and sister deep in the English countryside, I had no choice but to sing to anything that would listen. You see although I was sure that my dulcet tones were a joy to all who were lucky enough to be within hearing distance, my family felt differently! Oh yes, altogether differently! In fact, they tell me now that my singing was so appalling that the whole family would run into their various bedrooms and lock the doors. So what could this budding Maria Callas do? I had to continue my practising, even though nobody believed in me but me. But it can be hellish lonely going through life, if you're the only one who believes in you. But that shouldn't deter anyone from doggedly ploughing on, always keeping those dreams on course.

So I gave up on all those mere humans living their blind lives up at the house, and gave myself mind, heart, soul and voice to the farmyard. The poor chickens, ducks, geese, pigs, goats and ponies couldn't go into their rooms and lock the door. Admittedly I did corner them, or rather, they did try to run, but finally they surrendered to the white picket fence where I'd serenade them till dusk and the twittawoo of Owl Chorus . . . laughable really the image of this horrid little girl trapping innocent creatures against a white picket fence, forcing them to listen to 'Danny Boy' and 'Madam Butterfly'.

It didn't take me long to cotton on to the fact that my dearest friends in the world, my animals, were, or seemed to be, becoming cheesed off; and definitely let their feelings be known by rushing down to the picket fence, where they would proceed to quack, moo, snort, baa, neigh, hiss, bark, crow and cluck. How could any really brilliant talent compete with such a barrage of insults!

So, being determined, but not cruel, I had to find another audience for my singing practice; and this is how my eternal respect for trees began. Trees you see couldn't run away, they always seem to me to be so open, dignified, continuous, benevolent, seeing and hearing all. Have you ever put your arms around them and said a prayer? Try it. You see a tree has enormous energy and its branches go straight up to Heaven. If you happen to be the sort of child who doesn't believe in Heaven, just sit cross-legged at the foot of some beautiful old oak tree and feel its strength coming through your back and down your spine. Trees can also relieve headaches. Clasp your arms around them and hug them tight, putting your head against their bark . . . is she barking mad? Those of you who think this a fair old hoot and a load of old codswallop, try it and see. So, thanks to my dearest and bestest friends, my trees, my singing practice remained uninterrupted for quite a few years . . . until my Mother became so nervous that I was spending too much time singing to the trees and the animals, that she accused me of being a witch. I didn't know what a witch was, but the family thought it was serious enough for me to be sent away to a horrible posh boarding school with not an animal or tree in sight. This broke my heart, my spirit, destroying all aspiration, and what was worse – deadening all singing dreams. Black years ahead. Help!!

Angela Douglas

Time brings many things to my mind and my head is a muddle of woolly and half-digested memories, but I can remember with crystal clarity how I loved babies. 'Mummy, can I be a nanny when I grow up?' 'Never! you'll have enough to do, washing your own babies' nappies.' She'd say the words quickly in answer to my often repeated question, an incredulous expression in her eyes. I write now and try to describe what it meant to have determined parents, forever optimistic, who wanted something else for their daughter. Not *just* something else – they were more specific. They wanted me to become an actress. There was more than one occasion when the would-be nanny in me went hand in hand with the aspiring actress.

One of our neighbours had been married to an Indian and she had a beautiful baby boy of ten months. And I was trusted to take him to Hyde Park in his pram. Strapping him in, my mother shot me an anxious glance, reminding me to 'only cross on the crossings'.

Outside in the street I briskly pushed the pram, and in just holding the handle I began to feel the part. My back straightened. My head got higher. *My baby*. He was black and I wasn't. A fourteen-year-old with plaits, short socks, sandals and freckles. It was quite a walk to the Serpentine and since it was a weekday the park seemed almost deserted. I sat myself down on a bench beside two women – their heads bent in whispered conversation. I waited. I rocked the pram, coo-cooed and clucked. The women ceased to talk – they started to watch me. I could feel it. 'Dear little baby.' Her companion smiled in agreement.

'Ow, thankew sew much . . . isn't he the cutest thaing? He's ma furst *baby* an' ahm sew *threeled* with hym . . . he's the image of ma husband.'

The women sort of shifted on their bottoms and exchanged wide-eyed looks. Then they focused on *me*. The one nearest me pursed her lips and leaned forward moving her legs apart, planting her hands firmly on her knees. '*Gosh*,' I thought, 'I can see her knickers.'

She said rather crisply, '*Your* BABY? A *husband*? but you're so young!'

'Ah,' I pronounced. 'Ah, yes, wheel ya see, ahm from Tennessee.' I paused for maximum effect. 'The United

States, you know . . . we mayrrie verry early baack home.' In the silence of utter astonishment that followed, I smiled my sweetest isn't-life-wonderful smile and said 'Ma little one's goin' to need some lunch . . . ah think bottle feedin' *sew bad*, don't you?' And pulled my cardigan close together across my chest for emphasis. 'Goodbye, y'all,' I said without looking back.

I wonder, is it the memories we have of our childhood which influence us the most – and stay with us the longest?

Ronnie Barker

For Christmas 1933 I received, among other gifts, two tin aeroplanes. They were bi-planes, and one had real little lights on the upper wings, and the bulbs lit up by a battery.

Wonderful as they seemed to my five-year-old eyes, I still craved, but sadly did not receive the present that was nearest to my heart's desire; a 'Tiger Tim' annual. I received an 'Oojah' annual which, you must admit, comes pretty close; but not 'Tiger Tim'. Christmas came and went. At the beginning of March, my father came into the bedroom one morning (my mother was unwell at the time) and told me that he had a wonderful surprise for me. I knew straight away that my prayers had been answered, and rushed to hug him.

Imagine my disappointment when I found that all I had got was a baby sister.

Then, two years ago, in a junk shop, there it was. 'Tiger Tim's Annual'. I pounced on the dusty dog-eared delight and clasped it to me. At last it was mine, it had arrived.

Almost exactly fifty years late.

Pam Gems

Yesterday . . . a long time ago

I have sometimes wondered whether it is a nostalgia common to everyone which makes the past seem funnier than the present. In my own case it's probably something to do with winning a scholarship at the age of eleven, and being ejected from the bleak but warm surroundings of an extremely lowly existence. Somehow, before that time, there was a special sort of fun to be got out of life. A sort of freedom, though I daresay it was as much to do with being very young. I remember a Sunday School teacher called Mr Foster. A dear, kind man, who went about on an old bike, which he rode incredibly slowly (we fell off when we tried to copy him) with a spade tied along the bar – he had an allotment. One day during Bible Class a boy called Ernie stuck his head round the door and yelled 'Hey, Fossy, there's a horse on your bike!' and ran away. We thought it was just cheek but when we went outside it was true, the horse was lying down just by the steps; you couldn't see the bike. It belonged to a man called Rooky and it took ages to get up. Rooky said it was an Act of God, and Fossy, who was a saintly man, didn't make a case of it. He just left the bike where it was, a sort of flattened dish-shaped curve . . . you had to step over it, and you could see it from the road. Was it meant as a gentle reproach? If so it was wasted on Rooky, a local gyppo who wouldn't have recognized a reproach if it had been delivered by a Sherman tank.

Then there was the time we went carol singing and a woman asked if we knew anything about Ascot heaters. She was the cashier at the Home and Colonial and she would have sued, if she could have caught any of us after we blew her up. It might seem odd that she chose to appeal to ten year olds, but education was the thing in those days and there was respect by the olduns for us young ones . . . I see the same thing in Spain today.

One of my jobs, out of school, was to fetch and carry bags of coal for people. I had an old hoodless pram and could earn quite a bit for people too swanky, or too old or ill, bedridden or crippled with arthritis to get their own coal. I can't remember why they couldn't have the coal man deliver, I think there were sacks of cheap stuff you had to haul yourself. I took some to an old woman whose name I can't remember and she asked me to take her cat to the dispensary in my pram, she said it was ill. I knew the cat, a boring old greyish tabby. It looked terrible, and when I went to pick it up it was stiff, however, I took it. Some friends and I dressed it up in a doll's dress and bonnet and wheeled it about the town till the fun wore off. Then we didn't know what to do with it so, as my friend Phyl lived in a squalid dump at the back of the vicarage, we thought it might make a nice surprise for the vicar, so we left it on top of a box of groceries at the side door. I've often wondered what they thought and as I forgot to go back and explain to the old girl about her cat I expect she wondered too.

Then there was Neen. She ran the dry-cleaners, a new and fancy idea that took a few years to catch on in the town. She had three sisters, all married, but Neen was different. She was very bandy and thought she was Joan Crawford. She used to get very ratty if you didn't treat her with the proper star status, if you did she was very kind, we had a wonderful time out of it. She wore a red felt hat, winter and summer, with a black spotty veil, even in the shop. Sometimes she could be quite normal, so long as you didn't mention the silver screen or Miss C. In the end, amazingly, she married one of the Clark brothers, who were a good looking lot . . . I think he felt sorry for her. We were all invited . . . most of us couldn't go, not having the clothes, but we waited outside and suffocated her with confetti, this being allowed by the clergy in those days – labour was cheap. Neen wore red, naturally, with silver accessories, and looked a treat but for the legs. We all thought it was a romantic love story with a happy ending that she deserved, but her husband was killed in North Africa. As I remember she went about with a Pole for a while, but my mother told me the neighbours knocked that on the head.

My other favourite memory is of Miss Bellairs. She was a lady. There were a lot of them in those days, and the divisions were rigid. It was a rural area, so the middle class was thin on the ground. A doctor or a solicitor might be invited to lunch, never to dinner. We all had relations who worked in the big houses, so we knew what was what. Miss Bellairs' claim to fame to we children was her cousin, who had gone down in the Titanic. Bets were laid as to how often you could get her to mention it – any mention of the sea, boats, weather or travel would usually do the trick but you got extra points if you could bring her on by an abstruse comment about President Roosevelt (she once told me it was pronounced Rosevelt, not Roosevelt, but I thought she was gaga) or, say, ice cream, ice being the trigger word. She went about in a wheelchair, pushed by a companion, which had a silver vase on each wooden arm, filled with flowers, which she liked to bend and sniff while she was talking. Once my mother was chatting to her on Friar's Cliff, a favourite walk edged by heavy bracken in which we loved to play (we now know bracken dust to be highly carcenogenic!). Miss Bellairs was passing the time of day graciously when a goat's head appeared and ate her left-hand roses . . . Nobody seemed to notice but me. Its head then appeared on the right hand side but, being on a tether, it couldn't reach so I pushed the chair slightly to help him, causing the companion to draw back. The goat, baffled by this manoeuvre, ate the companion's skirt instead. She turned, the chair spun round, my mother was caught across the legs by their Pomeranian and fell, and the chair rolled slowly down the path with the companion, hampered by the goat having half her skirt down his throat, acting as a brake. My mother, swearing at the hole in her stocking, flew down the hill after them to assist, hoping for a shilling. However, they seemed to blame us and went off in a huff, so we lost the odd sub from that quarter.

In all, my memories of those days of poverty are shot

through with acts of kindness from individuals. It was through the kindness of the Relieving Officer, a lost generation wreck from the First World War who could never forgive himself for having survived when his friends died, and the local tailor who was chairman of the British Legion, that money was found for me to go to grammar school. It was the end of one world and the beginning of another. I don't say my troubles, which were many, were over, a great many began. But I know two things. I went hungry as a child and it's horrible. You think of nothing, nothing but food. And I found that education is a way out of slavery. You're no longer rubbish, to be discarded, to do as you're told, to shut up. You're allowed to have imagination. I once had a very rich young American friend, a beautiful girl, oddly enough, a god-daughter of President Roosevelt. She went to work for Shelter and they threw her out after several weeks. 'I don't understand it,' she said, 'all I did was say to these people, why do you have children when you can't afford it? And why don't you do something with this place, all it needs is a little love, some paint you can get at Woolworths, a few bright Indian spreads . . . just imagination!' And it was impossible to convey to her that imagination is forbidden for most people. It isn't encouraged, it isn't developed, neither is resourcefulness nor responsiveness to life. She was talking to crippled people and complaining of their inability to walk. It's alchemy, 'free' education, in my experience – the yellow brick road. I use the quotes because, of course, nothing is free. What *is* free, in a democracy, is the choice of how we spend our money. Good schools, fine teachers, for me, every time. People are our main natural resource. Precious.

Linda McCartney

For as long as I can remember I've been madly in love with horses and although it was my dearest wish, I never had the opportunity to own one until I got married.

As a child I would spend hours in a nearby riding school grooming horses and giving instruction in exchange for rides. As a result of this I was allowed to represent the stables in local horse shows and was eventually able to qualify for a competition in Madison Square Garden.

I rode a horse called Sunbeam in two classes and, although I didn't win anything, it was the most thrilling moment of my young life. I learned early that the taking part was more important than the winning.

Baroness Platt of Writtle, CBE
Chairman, Equal Opportunities Commission

Childhood, schooldays, happy days – how lucky I was with a secure home. All the disappointments of child-hood which seem so big at the time are absorbed in the end within a happy family life.

My earliest memory of school life was rushing down to the end of the school garden at break, aged four and a half, to search for conkers amongst the dry crackly leaves of the horse-chestnuts. Their mahogany sheen discovered amongst the blanket of leaves was to me as exciting as the glitter of real gold.

Later my most exciting discovery at school was of the pleasures of arithmetic. We had a most irascible retired headmaster who taught us mental arithmetic every morning. How grateful I am to him for teaching me how to work things out quickly in my head. 'Twelve herrings at three ha'pence' he would say pointing at you. Quick as a flash you said 'One and six'. Any suggestion of not being able to provide an immediate answer was unacceptable, and the blackboard rubber might fly across the room in your direction if you got it wrong. All this sounds like a pantomime to today's children – their life style is so different. Education has progressed, or has it? Certainly that old headmaster awakened a lifetime love of maths in me.

Later when I went to the Westcliff High School for Girls my maths mistress encouraged me and gave me extra lessons so that I was one of the first two girls from the school to achieve further mathematics for matric. My chemistry mistress let us go into the laboratories before school and in the dinner hour to grow enchanting lilac and purple alum crystals. Science was exciting too!

I remember being asked to help a girl to understand maths better during the Easter holidays, and at the end she gave me a pot of honey – much appreciated!

During the war our maths mistress gave us each 1 lb of wool and we had to knit an ounce a day during the Easter holidays, so that long navy blue scarves were sent off to keep sailors warm at sea.

Country dancing, guide camps, giggling at 'the pictures', swimming, reading, school plays all contributed to a kaleidoscope of rich experience. We were the lucky ones.

Dudley Moore

The first times that I ever performed are very hazy in my memory. I know that when I was about eleven I seemed to start playing a string of angels wearing rather cumbersome white wings made from all sorts of materials. Perhaps I looked rather cherubic in those days. Jonathan Miller certainly said when I was in *Beyond the Fringe* in London in 1960, that I struck him as a sort of 'grubby cherub' which I think was an analysis that was inevitable when one extrapolated certain features of my size, general disposition and fairly schoolboyish thought processes!

My mother tells me that she remembers my first performance as being a time when in front of a group of people . . . a group that has since become nebulous in memory, I performed a song, 'Little Sir Echo'. The only distinguishing feature from this otherwise fairly mediocre start to my show-business career was the fact that I insisted on singing the song while protected by the gaol-like bars of a chair. So there I was on stage standing behind a chair and probably holding on to the rods and peering out with tremulous eyes and voice.

I remember later on when I was about fifteen going

quite willingly out into the garden to show off my violin playing skills to Mrs Wilson, who lived in Number 148 Baron Road, in Dagenham, Essex – next door. I used to set up a music stand in the garden amongst the damp earth, snails, grass and rhubarb, then clothespeg my music (generally 'In a Monastery Garden') to a rather rickety music stand. I would then take my violin and play into the very non-resonant and non-sympathetic air, trying to stimulate Mrs Wilson's imagination to enter the Monastery garden of my making.

I don't think I had too much luck with my inspirational efforts!

Doris Stokes

The frock

As soon as I saw it I knew I had to have it. There it was in Sharples' window, the most beautiful frock in the world. Made of velvet, soft and plush as a kitten's fur and coloured the deepest, purest powder blue, it had gold braid round the collar and cuffs, a neat waist band and a full, graceful skirt.

Every day on my way to school I passed Sharples' window and every day I stood there gazing longingly at the frock. I would give anything, absolutely anything I decided, to own that frock.

At home I dropped outrageous hints and when that didn't work I abandoned all subtlety.

'D'you know the thing I want most in all the world?' I asked, although by now my parents were perfectly familiar with it. 'If I could have that blue velvet dress in Sharples window I'd never ask for anything else ever again.'

My parents seemed quite unmoved.

'Blue velvet dresses cost a lot of money,' my father used to say, 'We'll have to see Doll – won't we?'

Money was a big problem in the Sutton household. My father had been gassed in the First World War and couldn't work. My mother took in washing. There was never much cash to spare and whatever they had, my parents were just as likely to share with other people.

Gloomily I resigned myself to the fact that the most beautiful frock in the world would never be mine. Yet still I lingered outside Sharples' window.

And then one day I came out of school, dawdled up to Sharples and stopped dead in horror. The dress was gone.

It was the Friday before Whitsuntide and in those days people who could afford it quite often had new clothes for Whit Sunday. It was quite obvious that some lucky girl was having my beautiful blue velvet dress as a Whitsun present.

Miserably I wandered home, disappointment like a lead ball in my stomach. Against all the odds, even though I knew it was impossible, I'd secretly hoped that that dress would be mine. And now it was gone for ever.

I pushed open the door, scuffed into the house and for the second time that day stopped dead. There on the couch was a big bag with Sharples written across it. It was a very squashy bag. Squashy and soft, looking, for all the world as if it contained a velvet dress. I didn't dare go near it, didn't dare even look at it for fear I'd die of disappointment if it turned out to be some washing for Mum packed up in a fancy bag.

'Don't you want to know what's in that bag?' asked my father putting his head round the door.

I stared at him trying to read his expression.

He laughed, 'Go on. You can open it.'

I almost screamed with delight. That meant it was for me and that meant . . . I dived to the couch, tore open the bag, shredding the paper in my excitement and suddenly my fingers were sinking into velvet. Rich blue velvet.

Speechless with wonder I shook the dress free of the tattered bag and held it up to the light. It was even more beautiful close up than it had been in the window. I just knew it was going to make me look nice. I started to unbutton my cardigan.

'No,' said my mother firmly. 'You don't put that on till Sunday.'

My face fell but it was a gnat bite compared to the joy of owning the frock.

The dress was put reverently on to a hanger and several times a day, when my hands were clean I took it out of the cupboard for the sheer pleasure of gazing at it and stroking the gorgeous pile.

I counted the hours until Sunday but when the big day arrived it was raining.

'No,' said Mother. 'You're not wearing it in the rain and that's that. You'll ruin it.'

I argued, cried, pleaded but it was no use. I was forced

to sulk off to Sunday school in my threadbare Sunday best.

By the time I got back however, things looked much brighter. The rain had stopped, the clouds had lifted and there was a lemony-grey bit where the sun was trying to break through.

'Oh please, please,' I begged, 'please let me wear my dress.'

In the end they gave in. Father polished my black ankle shoes, I washed and changed into clean underwear and mother found me a pristine pair of socks. Then the dress was slipped over my head and suddenly I was transformed. Looking in the full-length mirror in my mother's wardrobe I saw a mysterious and elegant stranger vibrant in shimmering blue. I twirled and twirled and then I was off to show myself to the world.

With my coat over my arm in case of rain I hurried along to Wyndham Park. On Sunday afternoons when the weather was fine everyone went to Wyndham Park to stroll, to meet their friends and to watch the world go by. Well, today they could watch me.

I think I must have strutted every inch of the park that day, my head held high, convinced everyone was staring at me and admiring my dress. I felt wonderful. It was the most marvellous moment of my life.

Eventually the light began to fade and I realized it must be well past tea-time. Reluctantly I made my way home.

'Well Doll?' said Father when I got back, 'Was it worth it?'

'Oh yes, Father,' I assured him. 'It was wonderful. I felt like a queen!'

'Then you're a very lucky girl,' he said, smiling at my flushed face.

I took great care of my lovely frock, my pride and joy. But then months later my mother fell ill. She took a long time to recover and father said she would need extra fruit and milk and eggs to build her up.

'So you see, we've all got to make sacrifices to buy her things like that,' he went on, 'and I'm afraid I've got to sell your blue dress.'

I'm ashamed to say that instead of agreeing at once, I threw a tantrum. I flung myself onto the floor, I kicked and screamed and beat my fists. I deserved a soundly smacked bottom, but instead of hitting me, my father knelt quietly at my side.

'Listen to me Doll,' he said, 'What was it you said to me the night you came back from Wyndham Park, when I asked you was it worth it?'

'I don't know! I don't know!' I yelled.

'Well I remember,' he said, 'You said to me, "Father I felt like a queen." Now let me tell you something my girl. There are millions of people in this world who go from their cradle to their grave and never know one day or one hour when they felt like that. Nobody can take that away from you. Remember that. Nobody.'

And you know something? He was absolutely right. Blue velvet dresses don't last. Even when you get to keep them, they wear out or you grow out of them, but that wonderful, marvellous day when I felt like a queen, will last for ever in my memory. And the sight of rich blue velvet brings it flooding back . . .

Dame Jill Knight, DBE

Member of Parliament

I was about five years old. I had often been to the small corner shop with my mother and was struck by the fact that she never had to pay for the goods she bought. It was not explained to me (and I probably wouldn't have understood it if it had been) that my mother paid her bill every month. But I saw no sign of that – only the goods coming over the counter without any payment in return.

One day she asked me to go and get some cut ham for dinner and, proud of being given the responsibility for the errand, I trotted off happily. As I waited for the shopkeeper to slice the ham, my eyes were caught and riveted by a large bottle of jelly sweets. Oh the colours! Green, orange, yellow, red, purple – and I knew just how delicious each one would taste. I thought that since they were all free I would have some so, when the ham was cut, I asked in as grown-up a manner as I could for a bag of 'those'. The shopkeeper weighed them out, gave me the ham and the sweeties, and off I went.

As soon as I was outside the shop I knew I had done something wrong. I couldn't really figure out quite what it was but I knew I wasn't supposed to have those sweeties. I couldn't take them back. I didn't know what my mother would say when I got home with them. I couldn't possibly eat them all between the time I left the shop and the time I got home so I hit upon the plan of giving one away to each house and I solemnly put one sweetie on every doorstep as I passed. My mother never knew. The matter was never raised and I presume she just paid the bill without looking at it at the end of the month. But the feeling of guilt stopped me from sleeping much that night and never, ever, since have I been lured down the criminal path.

Muriel Spark

James Gillespie's School

James Gillespie, the founder of the school, died in 1797. He had been a tolerant, frugal but benevolent bachelor. He made his large fortune out of snuff-making, and in the true Edinburgh style, left it to the City, in the form of a foundation for old people and one for a school. Both were later to be merged into an educational foundation.

So it was that parents, like my own, of slender means but high aspirations were able to send their children to Gillespie's, at a moderate fee. In a charming school-house on Bruntsfield Links I spent the whole of my schooldays, from the age of five in 1923 to that of seventeen in 1935. At first, during my schooldays, it was co-educational, but after some years we lost our little boys, and we were James Gillespie's High School for Girls.

Since this was the only school I ever attended it would be useless to deny that it bears some resemblance to any other Edinburgh school that I may happen to have described in a novel. But my debt to Gillespie's is far greater than that due to a formal setting for a work of fiction.

I was not aware of it then, but now I know that this school was remarkably in advance of its time. It was in many respects a progressive school. Our teachers were serious and often very humorous. Most of them were women of the generation who had lost their sweethearts in the First World War. They preached the evils of war. We girls, in our blue gym tunics and dark red blazers with the golden unicorn crest, were encouraged to the best of our capacities to benefit from our education, to know something, do something with our lives, and above all do something for others outside of ourselves. We were taught to think. In my education at this school, thinking was doing. I hope it still is, and that the Scottish virtue of perseverance is still conveyed in the educational system.

My recollections of twelve years' constant attendance, less the necessary absence for the measles, are extremely vivid. I made a few friends in each class, but I had one special friend throughout my schooldays, a lover of poetry and literature like me. We composed stories together and tried out on each other our first poems. My first poem, at the age of nine, was an improved version of Robert Browning's *The Pied Piper*.

There were a few men teachers. I recall our singing master, a Mr Wishart, who cheerfully managed to get tuneful songs out of us and who taught us the rudiments of music. There was an art master, Arthur Cooling, himself an artist, who was an object of infinite glamour to us all. I forget the name of our history master, but remember well his passion for the industrial revolution, and the fact that he made me sit at the front of the class so that he could stroke my hair while teaching, an innocent occupation which made the other girls titter quite a lot.

But above all, there was a Miss Christina Kay under whose influence I came when I was about eleven. Some people who were at school with me have identified her with my character Miss Brodie, but I can assure you that no character of fiction could ever compete with Christina Kay. Indeed, if it were possible that the two women could have met, Miss Kay would have put Miss Brodie firmly in her place. To Miss Kay's teaching, her opening up to us of the imaginative life of art and literature, her encouragement of any talent she could find, my debt is very great. I never really had a choice of profession. Christina Kay predicted for me a literary future, and that was the end of the story, full stop.

I was born and brought up nearby, in Bruntsfield Place, and used to walk to school through the beautiful Bruntsfield Links which I loved in all seasons. They were my first playground, including the golf course and the putting green in the long summer evenings of our country. In my teens I used to come to school particularly early, 7.30 or 8.00 in the morning, often through the snow, to be in time for an extra-curriculum class in Greek; this was taught to three girls as a special concession by a charming classics teacher, Miss Munroe, who looked like a pre-Raphaelite painting.

After school I would make straight for the public library. Those free libraries of Edinburgh – what would we have done without them? The Border Ballads were my favourite reading. I read the unsurpassably beautiful Bible. Sir Walter Scott was required reading, and although I never took to his prose, I got from him a sense of living history and the imaginative realization of being part of it. The senior school had a gifted English teacher, Alison Foster, who put English literature our way far beyond what was necessary for us merely to take our exams. To me, those were inspiring days.

Muriel Spark, *Reading* 1988 (Text taken from a lecture delivered by the author to the United Kingdom Reading Association).

Julian Pettifer

'Having a ball'

I have never understood why that intrusive Americanism 'having a ball' should have been so enthusiastically adopted over here as an exchangeable term for having a good time. I've been to some pretty awful balls over the years, but not one of them was half as ghastly as the very first.

To be fair, it wasn't the ball itself that was to blame; it was just that I was painfully shy, gauche and wholly ill-prepared for such a social occasion. At the time I think I was eleven years old and it must have been at the beginning of the Christmas holidays when an invitation arrived from a prep. school friend to a Junior Hunt Ball. I had only the vaguest notion about such events, but everything I knew suggested it was not for me. Confined as I was within the cast-iron monasticism of the prep. school system of those days, to say that I was inexperienced with girls is seriously to understate the position. My attitude towards girls was similar to – and probably partly modelled on – the views that William Brown of the 'Just William' stories held of Violet Elizabeth Bott. It was compounded of fear and contempt; but mostly fear. Hence, if it is accepted that the first object of going to a ball is to mingle with the opposite sex, I was clearly not going to be a very good mingler; and if it is further accepted that the second object of attending a ball is to dance, then my credentials were even shakier. At that point in my life I had never had a single dancing lesson and my only attendance upon the Terpsichorean Muse had seen me, as a mixed infant, skipping around the maypole to the rousing strains of 'Here we go gathering nuts in May'.

That experience apart, I was wholly ignorant. Asked to cut a rug, I should have reached for the garden shears. I did not know the one-step from the two-step, the waltz from the foxtrot, the round dance from the square dance, or the belly dance from the Highland fling.

'Never mind,' Mother said, 'I will teach you.' Why she wanted me to go to that damned ball I shall never know, but she must have wanted quite badly because all my objections were over-ruled. The carpet was rolled back and she and I slow-slow-quick-quick-slowed around the drawing room to the strains of scratchy 78 rpm records.

The invitation had stated 'Black tie', but what was I to wear? Something of my older brother's could be cut down. Of course. My heavy heart plunged a few more fathoms and when the chopped-down garments came back from the 'little woman' who made our curtains, my cup of misery was full. The jacket was too long and the trousers were too short and bagged grotesquely at the knees.

As the ball drew nearer my terror grew daily, but even the nightmares of those restless nights were light entertainment compared with the real thing. I can only recall two mental and physical states: I was either pale and sick with fright or puce and sick with embarrassment. I lurked in corners trying to hide my ghastly suit. I locked myself in the loo until people rattled on the door and shouted rude words. Even when they announced the buffet supper, I was too queasy to eat.

My eventual salvation came when a loud, bosomy lady in a black sequined dress asked me to help out by carrying trays of drinks to the adults who were enjoying themselves in an adjoining room. Things instantly got better. To begin with, I soon felt I was being treated as a servant, which was a huge improvement on my being the cloddish guest.

Next, I discovered that the trays of drinks I was transporting contained much more interesting beverages than the ones being served to the junior hunts persons. As I returned to the billiard room for refills, I began to sample those colourful and forbidden glasses: a sip of Pimms, a taste of gin and It, a sup of cider cup, a mouthful of sherry. I began to feel better. I too would cut the rug. Which I did – until the moment I threw up all over it, a priceless Persian rug. If that is 'having a ball', I bet my hostess wished she hadn't.

Toyah Willcox

Most of my entries in my school diary are the same. What jokes I played on whom, and how badly I behaved in classes. I found my schooldays too protected and frustrating. I was a difficult pupil to say the least, but my education sadly lacked humour. I often feel if this had been present in my schooling it might have taken the edge off my bad behaviour.

I am now twenty-eight years old and value education highly. I don't think education should ever end, but it is only in recent years that I have become ready and willing to be educated. I will seek this for the rest of my life.

Here are some extracts from my 1972 diary when I was thirteen years old and went to an all girls' school:

January 11th Tues
Started school, yuk!
Dad goes back to hospital [Dad cut the main artery in his right hand on a broken glass].
All the rules have been changed. Vicky Richardson and I are in charge of books (how boring). Lessons are still boring.

January 12th
Got into trouble with Idle for being in the activity room instead of lessons. Nearly got into trouble with Bory for swearing at Sally in netball, she kept knocking the ball out of my hands. In needlework I'm making a jacket out of my own design.

January 13th
Boring wet day! In Break we played strip Jack naked. I was left with few clothes on in the form room. Vicky, Wendy and I played strip Jack naked again behind the main stage curtain in the assembly hall. Wendy was left in bra and pants. Marc Bolan was on 'Magpie'.

February 16th
We had a church service today. We had the preacher who dropped his false teeth two years ago. In history I got sent out, but I kept going back to ask for my horror book back, which had been confiscated; the words that were shouted at me! I passed my maths, history and biology tests.

February 23rd
School, yuk!
Started cookery today. Talked about boys all day.

February 29th
All lessons are boring!
I had my singing lesson with Mrs Cull, she was very pleased with me because my voice has improved a lot. I got in trouble in English.

March 7th
I'm starting a strict diet. I worked hard all morning. In afternoon break I attacked Sally, she left two teeth marks in my arm. We had a maths test. Confirmation class was fun. I blew my nose in my hand by mistake. I enrolled in theatre school.

I wrote this poem in recent years about the frustration
I felt at having to go to school:

Growing pains

She didn't hear a word
As mother drove her
Home from school.
Her little head lost
Deep in a starlit pool.

And the breeze
    Through the leaves
        Of the trees
            Through the window
                Kept her face cool.

And her mother rambled on,
That father that afternoon
Had been a right fool.
Brought down the greenhouse
With some new fandangled pneumatic tool.
'You're quiet dear, bad day at school?'
And she looks in vain
For stars in a summer sky.

Held by chains
    And too tired to cry,
As tears form
    In her shining eyes,
Searching so hard
    For signs of life
Is she insane
    Or is it growing pains?

To keep cutting the sky
      With a questioning knife?
Old enough to realize
She's living a lie.

Needing an earth bound observer to untie
All the knots in her head.
'Are you all right?
      Dear, perhaps you should go early to bed!'

She still doesn't reply.
Here we are
Under a vast alien sky,
Wondering if we're nothing more
Than time's passers by.

Liz Rigbey

Producer, The Archers

My parents took us to Bournemouth for the day when I was four. It was typical seaside weather, and we all wore lots of jumpers. My family sheltered from the wind and picked sand out of the sandwiches while I played nearby, yes, I'm afraid almost certainly with a bucket and spade.

Two men walked past me. I think now they were probably father and son. One was telling the other about crabs. ('Crabs walk sideways. They have eight legs and if one of these legs is hurt, a crab doesn't sit around howling for an elastoplast: it just breaks off the leg and

116

walks away without it. Then it grows a new one.') I had to know more. I forgot bucket, spade and family and set off behind the men, close enough to hear what they were saying. '(As a young crab gets older it grows out of its skin, just the way you grow out of your clothes. Crabs don't live in holes or houses: they have hard shells instead.' Past shouting children and huddled family groups, we picked our way round sandcastles and up the steps to the promenade. ('Crabs have babies by laying eggs, millions of them, which float away in the sea and grow up somewhere else. They never see their parents again.')

The two men suddenly disappeared into a beach hut. I realized I was lost. I wandered about looking for familiar faces and was soon even more lost. The long row of identical beach huts stretched out before me. I couldn't even remember which one the men had gone into.

The rest of this story is fairly predictable. Child wanders into nearest beach hut. Child's parents sought in vain by kind holidaymakers. Child is taken to police station where she is taught some new nursery rhymes. Meanwhile, parents frantically comb the beach, search parties formed, swimmers seek child's body in sea, mother heard to pray for the first time ever, brother in tears etc. Pale-faced father eventually reclaims jolly child from police station and finds she has a thing or two to tell him about crabs. Crabs rapidly assume status of unmentionable subject in family household.

What a shame my parents had to suffer such distress while their daughter learned a few tricks she would try to employ herself twenty-five years later: that is, the art of making the listener want to hear more.

Irene Handl

Pretty little May gets 20 years hard

When I was a child I was convinced that Cockneys came in one of two types. Stout parties of jolly temperament and scarlet-and-blue complexions, who spoke in husky tones and swam in a fruity aura reminiscent of Christmas pudding. Or sharp-featured coves of incredible knowingness. Dark and slender, the coves were mostly costermongers. They were reputed to be of Spanish or Egyptian ancestry which was supposed to account for their elegant hands and feet.

The females of both parties shared these characteristics, except the incidence of Christmas pudding wasn't quite as high.

But I never really met a Cockney until I was nearly eight, and when I did there was absolutely no rapport.

The occasion was a Christmas treat my school was giving for the local board school, which was situated at the 'common' end of Maida Vale. So common, that, though nobody mentioned it, it was practically in the Harrow Road!

The children were marshalled into the hall by prison-warder-like teachers; even the women teachers seemed to my eyes of unparalleled ferocity.

They filed in with a thunderous noise (due, it was rumoured, to borrowed boots).

There were boys there, too. (Board schools are *mixed* we had been warned.)

At a word of command, they lined up to the tables, drew out their chairs, sat down. After Grace was said and their teachers served, they were given the sign to fall to.

We didn't take our tea with them, of course. Nor were we required to assist them with theirs.

Reproduced from the *London Evening News*, July 20, 1974.

Manners

They were waited-on grudgingly by our caretakers, stout parties both, who (not so privately) opined that these 'ere liberal carryings-on were high-falutin' rubbish.

I remember being rather disappointed that there was no major breach of manners. No one stretched across the table to grab a bun, or blew on their tea.

In fact, such a high state of gentility obtained that nobody dared to 'ask' and there were the inevitable 'puddles' from the mixed infants.

These were mopped up with glum resignation by the caretaker and his wife, for whom the pools were the natural outcome of goings on.

The high spot of the party came after tea when crackers were pulled (paperhats only! No whistles to be blown in the hall!) and presents handed out.

A dip in the bran tub unearthed a celluloid toy for each, to which an orange, a bun, and a paper bag of sweets were added.

Everyone – boys, girls, old men of the sea, *everyone* received a new penny. It was almost too much. They were marched out into the December gloom in a state of euphoria.

My next encounter was far more realistic, and exploded the Coves v Stout Parties theory for good.

I met a pretty little girl called May. May was a 'step girl'.

'Step girls' and 'Saturday girls' were quite frequent in those days. So were Saturday boys. They did the boots and the knives with a cork or emery powder on the knifeboard.

Both put the shillings they earned straight into the family budget.

Cooks of infirm spirit allowed their step girls warm water in cold weather, while knowing for a fact that stone didn't come up anything like as white as with cold water.

But I don't want to trespass on Margaret Powell territory. Enough that our cook was weak, that she pitied May's hands. Always blue and red, they turned a rewarding yellow when the chilblains burst.

Cook approved of May. My family approved of May. What's more, my family approved of May's family.

And May, as it happened, was for me. We climbed on to the garage roof, which was quite embowered in lilac. Like every other garage in St John's Wood, ours was an ex-coach house.

Sharing

When I was twelve and May fourteen I left her, or rather she left me, to be a general – in service, of course.

I was a bit huffy but May seemed quite delighted at the prospect of doing what could quite easily turn out to be 20 years' hard.

I never heard how she got on. I never asked. I didn't want to know what May was making of a life she wasn't sharing with me.

And anyway in two years the Great War broke out and everyone went into munitions. By the time the Armistice came along there was no such thing as the Great Domestic Problem in all the civilized world.

Still, I hope as long as I last there'll be Cockneys in London. Real Cockneys, I mean.

Bob Hoskins

One story that my mother often relates, concerns me at a Christmas party when I was about three years old. The story is funniest when you consider that I was a tough little boy and in my professional life I have often played as a gangster or a tough guy.

It was at a Christmas party, at my aunt's. She ran a boarding house at Southend on Sea. There were six children at the party, five girls and me, all under the age of six years. On Christmas day the children were very excited, talking all day about the children's party being held that evening and of their beautiful dresses they intended to wear. I was the youngest of the party and looked forward to what I was going to wear. When the time came to dress for the party, my mother started dressing me with a little sailor suit. When I realized that I was not having a party dress, I screamed the house down and would not stop until one of the girls' mothers offered to loan me a dress. At the party I was as happy as a sandboy. You can imagine what I looked like. At

that time it was fashionable for little boys to have crew cut haircuts. I looked like a miniature action man in drag!

My mother who was a nursery school teacher, often relates some of the funny things that have happened in her school. The children, all little Cockneys, under five years of age, rehearsed a passion play, to be played in front of their parents on Christmas eve. On the big day with all the mothers anxiously watching, the play came to a halt when the boy playing Joseph, forgot his lines. After several promptings, he became red faced and furious. He tore off his costume and in a very loud voice said,

'I didn't want to play F---ing Joseph in the first place.'

Lord King of Wartnaby

Chairman, British Airways

When I was around twelve years old, I was quite pleased with myself when I had half-a-crown in my pocket. As it happened, I had been dismissed from the school choir a week earlier for minor misdemeanours. I was therefore on my best behaviour as I took my place in church the following Sunday morning. I assumed what I hoped was a suitably other-worldly expression.

I contrived to keep in place the halo of distracted benevolence until the time of the collection, and when the sidesman passed the plate around I plunged my hand into my pocket and retrieved and deposited on the plate the only coin which I found there. The halo disappeared very quickly when I noticed among the copper on the retreating plate the gleam of a single silver coin. I realized with dismay that I had parted company with the whole of my accumulated capital.

After the service I marched round to the vestry and explained to the Vicar that I believed that his collection would be found to contain a certain silver coin. The Vicar confirmed that indeed the collection had acceptably included one silver half-crown. I informed the Vicar that the 2/6d was my own and valued property and was intended as a deposit against my normal contribution which I had been unable to make because I had no other coins in my pocket, and had been most unwilling to incur any further displeasure from parental or ecclesiastical authority by making no offertory contribution. The Vicar asked me how much change I wished to have. I promptly replied 2/5d.

You may think that this story supports the contention that the child is father of the man.

Duke of Bedford

I wish I had those happy memories of childhood with the loving father and mother and the days full of laughter, companionship and fun with my brother and sister. I read about such families with envy.

My father had a hot line to God and neither of them seemed to have any heart at all. The only thing he liked was parakeets, who had heated aviaries and imported fruit. We lived in freezing houses and ate wormy apples from the orchard. My mother was a great one for fresh air and exercise and we lived in a constant draught or pursued foxes on snowy days on horseback or I was sent to be punched by boxing instructors who threw a bucket of icy water over me in mid-winter after the lesson was over.

We were brought up really by servants and scarcely saw our parents at all. When I was about fifteen my parents had a messy legal separation and each one had their own house. My mother went to live with her open windows and my father with a harem of hangers-on pushing his latest version of God's word and various bizarre political and financial schemes to save the world. During the war he was a pacifist and when he got up to speak in the House of Lords he could empty the chamber quicker than an air raid alert.

I remember the kindness and hospitality of neighbours and the staff who worked for us with deep gratitude, but otherwise childhood was something that I hated and life only became worthwhile when it was over. I never knew my parents, never had a conversation and never remember a single affectionate gesture though we lived under the same roof. All human emotion was deep frozen. Childhood was a waste of time, sad and lonely. Thank God it's over.

The Marquess of Bath

Schooldays, as far as my memory can recall, were not only living purgatory to me, but also to that wretched band of teachers who were entrusted with my education. It fell upon them the unenviable task of trying to instil knowledge into a complete moron, who was not only incapable of receiving it, but had no intention of aiding them in their designated duty.

I failed, as was expected, my Common Entrance Examination to Eton, a school that my family had always attended, so completely that no means of bribery or corruption could make the then 'Headmaster' relent and accept me as a pupil. Thank God, for my father's sake, Harrow was a different kettle of fish.

At that time, I'm afraid, it was not the highly regarded educational establishment that it is today. It was in fact, snobbishly considered to be rather common, and even, horror upon horrors, had a black boy as a student. To be requested to take the son of a Marquess who himself was a Viscount, no matter how dense he might have been, to them was a coup which I fear they were unable to refuse.

My time at Harrow was relatively uneventful, barring the fact that I broke my nose whilst playing football, a game that I was never very fond of. This minor accident was to leave me with a facial trademark for the rest of my life. I have never quite made up my mind whether this really turned out to be a blessing in disguise or not. My ancestors have always been renowned for their hawkish features, a distinguished appearance that was changed in a second, by one inopportune tackle.

In all other aspects, I feel my memories of Harrow are stronger on my behind than on my mind. I was beaten twice during my term of incarceration there, and the experience remains painfully with me to this day, though the cause of this punishment, I have long since forgotten. I know it is unfair, but when one looks back on one's childhood, summer holidays were always sunny whilst schooldays were fraught with cold and chastisement.

On leaving Harrow, which on my part I did with the utmost haste and relief, my parents sent me to a crammer in Norfolk in order to reach a level in my supposed education, to enable me to pass the examination into Christchurch, Oxford. To my amazement, let alone everyone else's, this I managed to do. I decided to study Agriculture for three very basic reasons. Firstly it required little or no brain; secondly it was the most interesting pursuit that was then on offer; and thirdly one was permitted a car in one's first year in order to get to the farm. This was by far the most important factor to me, as it gave one that longed for independence that educational establishments seem determined to deprive one of.

I succeeded in passing the Preliminary Exams, again to everybody's amazement, and promptly left Oxford with the mistaken belief that I was casting the shackles of educational stress from my legs forever.

No – I cannot say that my schooldays were happy ones, but I do admit that the fault was probably more my own than that of others. I happened, through no intention of my own, to be born prematurely but in every other phase of my life, I have always been late.

Growing up was the main unfortunate recipient of this unintentional tardiness. On considering my scholastic failures, one other supposition comes to mind. My greatest friend and mentor throughout my childhood and early youth, was a family gamekeeper named Dick Futcher. He was totally illiterate, yet to him I owe any intelligence that one day I may be accredited with. He taught me nature and eradicated pomposity. He was, and in my mind still is, my true companion. As I have said, he was uneducated, and maybe I felt that what was good enough for him, was good enough for me.

On the other hand, my children's schooldays were extremely happy ones, not for them but for myself. Peace would once again descend upon life and home, only to be marred by the horrendous school fees that regularly arrived, and painfully had to be paid. Actually I did this without too much remorse for, not only did it ensure their continued education, but it also guaranteed those glorious periods of total tranquillity in my daily existence. My own schooldays seem never to have ceased, and even to this present day, linear decimalization is involving me in no end of mental anguish. As in the past, my mind still totally fails to grasp this new indoctrination. One hundred centimetres has the same effect upon the comprehension as a mathematical debate with Albert Einstein would have had upon me. I will still keep trying, even though the chances of success are remote, but then, I suppose I am not that sort of person who, when given an inch, will take 1.6 kilometres!

Margaret Drabble

All I can remember clearly are terrible things like the Day the Cat Died, or the Day the Goldfish Jumped out of its Tank, or the Day I fell off the Pony. Childhood in recollection seems to be an endless succession of tragedies and humiliations, but I don't suppose it can have been *quite* so bad. For instance, I used to enjoy the pantomime at the Lyceum in Sheffield.

We all used to go, dressed in our best, and sit in a row in the stalls, and I loved it all – the chorus girls with their dazzling bright brown faces and their flashing teeth, the comics (whom I could never understand, but never mind, probably just as well), the songs and song sheets, the wonderful principal boy in fishnet tights and a pink bathing costume, the dame, the transformation scene, the flying ballet . . . I used to long for it *never to end*. I used to try to make it last longer, I wanted to stay there all year, in my little red velvet handed-down-from-big-sister-and-cousin-Sybil party dress. The only thing I didn't like was when children from the audience were asked to go on stage. That terrified me. How could they dare go up there and sing 'Mares Eat Oats and Does Eat Oats', while everybody laughed? And I didn't like it much when one of the comedians gave my little brother a huge balloon. He didn't like it either. He howled and I blushed. But on balance, the pantomimes were wonderful. I'd like to think that children still find them as wonderful and magical as I did.

Keith Waterhouse

Underneath the lamplight

I had a nasty shock the other day. I went back to the street where I was brought up and found that the lamp-post was missing.

There was a lamp-post there all right, a concrete clothes-prop fizzing pale-blue mercury and bathing the neighbourhood in shadowless light – very efficient, and for those within its pale orbit undoubtedly the next best thing to having a council house in the Sea of Tranquillity.

But the lamp-post I remember, *the* lamp-post – a squat, cast-iron pillar painted bright green, surmounted by a hissing gas-lantern that flickered behind four square window panes like a stranded lighthouse – was gone for ever. This is my requiem for it.

You must understand that it was more than a source of light. Our lamp-post was, to begin with, a highly functional object. Protruding from its iron neck was a stout metal bar, the official purpose of which was to support the ladder of the man who came to mend or clean the gas-mantle.

This metal bar was perfect for tying bits of rope to, swinging from, doing somersaults over, throwing pieces of slate at, or merely dangling from by two puny arms while your friends counted slowly to a hundred and you felt that you were on the rack.

Because of its basic usefulness to us the lamp-post was the pivot of our community. It was our maypole, roundabout, assault course, market place, moot and general headquarters.

It was the wicket for our cricket matches, one side of a goal mouth, the base of rounders and a complicated game called 'Relieve-oh!' which rarely got further than a shrill quarrel about its devious local rules.

We played marbles under our lamp-post, tested our conkers against its hollow, clanking base and shinned up it to light Woodbines and sparklers, or merely to experience the heady smell of singed hair.

The fraternity of our lamp-post, like an officers' mess or a gentleman's club, had a rigid system of protocol. No one was admitted to membership under the age of three; no one from other streets was allowed except as a guest; cry-babies, boy scouts and anyone wearing glasses were rigorously blackballed.

Ladies' night was on Fridays, when the girls of the street, hungry for adventure, hung about under that shining orb like tiny Lili Marlenes.

Our lamp-post was the venue for all the main social events of the year.

In high summer we sat beneath it poking tar bubbles in the road with long sticks or trying to prise up the lid of the storm-drain that was supposed to give you scarlet fever.

In November we assembled around it to count our fireworks and decide whether the Big Banger or the Jumping Cracker should be poked through Old Mother Teaker's letter box.

At Christmas we used it as a boundary post to divide the carol-singing concession between those whose voices had broken and those who could still bring a fine treble to the first two lines of 'Away in a Manger'. But the social attraction of the year in our street was the Button Fair, and this was invariably staged beneath our lamp-post. This always followed the annual bank holiday fair that was held on an acre of waste-ground near by; having lost all our pennies on the roll-'em-down stalls we would hurry home and chalk up our own stalls on the pavement, using buttons for money.

Different kinds of buttons had different values: a trouser button was the lowest denomination, a jacket button was worth two trouser buttons, an overcoat button was worth three, and a cloth-covered button snipped surreptitiously off your sister's best coat was worth four or even six for a big one.

Sometimes urchins from other streets tried to gate-crash the Button Fair with handfuls of shirt-buttons snitched from their mothers' work-boxes, but these were rejected as being worthless foreign currency.

If you had comics to swop at any time of the year, you stood under the lamp-post with your rolled-up merchandise tucked into your stocking; eventually a fellow-trader would come out with his stock of *Radio Funs* or *Knock-Outs* and haggle with you – one *Knock-Out* for two American Dick Tracy comics (they were a drug on the market at that time), or one *Radio Fun*, mint condition, for an incomplete copy of *Illustrated Chips* and a cigarette card of Don Bradman.

The best time around our lamp-post was on autumn evenings, after the rain. You looked gloomily out of the window, tired of Meccano and Dinky toys and craving human company. You'd see the gas-jet flicker and go on magically, by itself; its bouncing reflection would light up the puddles and tell you that the rain had stopped.

132

Out of the shadows would stroll some boy from up the street, looking about him, eager for companionship.

You'd watch him loafing around under the lamp-post and pray that he wouldn't go indoors again before you'd struggled into your raincoat. You'd hurry out and hang about with him, abstractedly discussing sex or football or floating a matchbox down the gutter, but all the time keeping a sharp look-out on the doors for signs of life.

Soon other figures would emerge from the shadows, and soon after that the whole street would be alive with boys: diving through the wet privet hedges, swinging like Tarzan from the iron bar of the lamp-post, whooping and whistling and yodelling, running in and out of that friendly pool of light.

As I said, our lamp-post has disappeared now. The concrete column that replaced it is far more serviceable and it probably holds a silver medal from the Road Safety Council. But there were no children playing beneath it when I passed. Where were they, I wonder? Watching television, or doing homework, or joining in constructive games in an adventure playground?

Has the magic gone out of childhood – or is it just that my generation were lucky possessors of a magic lamp?

From *Waterhouse at Large* (Michael Joseph Ltd)

Marjorie Proops

Beer. Everytime I walk past the open door of a pub, the pungent smell of beer evokes memories of my childhood.

Then I remember the sound of it, hissing from the bar pull, plopping into the glasses, frothy head rising, sometimes rising too fast, irritating to my father – pulling the pint – but deeply fascinating to my sister and me.

Other kids, she and I agreed, discussing our early days, remembered childhood scents of mown grass, syringa hedges or spring flowers in the park.

We remembered the smell of beer and it was, for us, a good, confident, reassuring smell. The smell of home. Our home was the flat above the pub.

Our dad was the landlord, our mother chief barmaid and washer up, smiling warmly at the customers as my father cracked appalling jokes and muttered out of the side of his mouth 'Get upstairs you two, right out of the bar, or else . . .'

We loved being in the bar not simply because it was forbidden territory but because it made our childhood much, much more exciting and interesting than that of our friends.

We reckoned their lives must be terribly boring. Not like ours, colourful and exotic.

Take the Guinness Girls for example. They came in every morning as the doors opened, wearing dusty black, shapeless garments, with tatty bits of fur round their necks in winter, and winter or summer, bashed up feathered hats jammed on their heads.

Invariably, they ordered their Guinness and settling their bottoms on the Windsor chairs, they would gossip and yarn the morning away as they sipped their good brown stout.

'Must look after my Guinness Girls,' our dad would say, making flirtatious little remarks to them as they appreciatively nodded their amazing headgear at him.

Our pub was in the City of London. We children thought our street had the prettiest name in town: Shepherdess Walk.

Pretty as it sounded, in reality it did not have a great deal of charm. Bucolic it was not. We grew up learning about life as it was in a hard, working-class neighbourhood.

We went to school at the redbrick Council at the end of the street.

We quickly discovered that there was one law for the poor and another for the less poor, typified by the class structure of the Saloon and Public Bars.

Customers in the Saloon bar usually drank shorts; whisky, or gin, out of a highly-polished glass. Those in the Public gulped beer out of thick glasses, dunked, but not dried. 'How unfair,' we would yelp.

'In this life,' said our philosopher father, 'you get what you pay for. Remember that, you girls. And to be able to pay, you have to work hard and do your lessons and your homework and make something of yourselves. *And get out of the bar!'*

Our mother did her best to put a finishing touch of refinement to our heady upbringing.

They were a great combination, our parents. A team working together to give their little girls love and security and a deep sense of reality of life in Shepherdess Walk.

It may not have been a storybook childhood. But neither my sister nor I would have changed a moment of it.

Funny, though. Neither of us can abide the smell of beer.

Michael Palin

My first stage appearance nearly put me off treading the boards for life. I was six or seven years old and my mother had taken me to the matinee of a variety show on the Cromer Pier. I remember being deeply impressed by the number of seats in the auditorium, most of them unoccupied, sitting in long, curving, neat rows.

On stage a blindfolded conjuror was being handed large steel rings which he cleverly and inexplicably wove together. I was less interested in the conjuror than I was in his assistant, a tall, glittering lady with long legs and a spangled costume. She had developed a graceful, but rather complex routine with the rings which she would execute deftly before handing each one to the conjuror.

The routine finished with a flourish from the man on the Hammond organ, and then my moment came. The conjuror, perspiring slightly, removed his blindfold, stepped forward and asked for a volunteer from the audience to hand him the rings. I didn't even wait to think about it. My hand shot up and I was halfway down the aisle before he even noticed me.

136

The next thing I knew I was climbing the steps on to the stage of the Cromer Pier Pavilion. All I had to do now was get it right. The music started. For a moment I hesitated then I remembered the turns, the swirls – everything the conjuror's assistant had done came back to me. I gave him the first ring, which I noticed that he grabbed rather sharply; after some more of the routine I gave him the second, which he took even more brusquely. By now I was carried away, wallowing unashamedly in the sheer delight of being part of a stage show. My third delivery climaxed a truly magnificent piece of twiddling and twirling. Flushed with happiness I finally delivered the ring, and the conjuror leaned down to me as he took it and through clenched teeth hissed the immortal words: 'For *Christ's* sake, stop muckin' about!'

I just gave him the next two rings straight, and he bowed and was duly applauded, and I went back to my seat having learnt, the hard way, my first lesson in upstaging.

Neil McIntosh

Director, Voluntary Service Overseas

Midnight may seem a pretty commonplace time to adult city dwellers. To a pair of eight-year-old boys in a small East Coast Scottish town the witching hour was just that

– a time, we assumed, when everything would be transformed, would *feel* different, a time therefore that we were certainly not permitted to experience.

We resolved to see for ourselves just how alien midnight might be. For some reason (perhaps because he was a vital five months older) my friend David agreed to get up first and come the few doors to my house where the time-honoured device of a piece of string, which went from the garden all the way up to where it was tied to my big toe, would wake me up.

It worked! I dressed and silently joined David, who was standing shivering slightly in the shrubbery at the side of our garden. The streets were utterly deserted with that intense quiet which is so special and so rare in the middle of a town.

We walked a little way. We heard footsteps like footsteps you might hear in a thriller made in black and white at Ealing Studios. For this was the mid-1950s and, in retrospect, I remember those midnight streets in monochrome.

The steps were those of a policeman, the black and white check band round his cap just visible as we crouched behind a low garden wall. We waited some minutes and then began to realize that midnight meant nothingness – the removal of all the diversions of the day which made life interesting. We made for home, and said goodnight and I tiptoed up the steps for the front door. It was locked!

Momentary panic was controlled by the memory of the bathroom window – always open and accessible by climbing a wall and traversing a low roof. I had done it dozens of times in the day and was to use it frequently, returning late after teenage parties. On this first nocturnal climb the haven of the bathroom was reached in a few minutes.

Just as I closed the window I heard my parents' bedroom door open. I guiltily pulled the chain just as my father switched on the bathroom light and started back slightly as he saw me. 'Goodnight, Dad,' I said and slipped past as he rubbed his eyes blearily.

It seemed to take hours to get to sleep but I was not disturbed again. Over breakfast my father suddenly stopped eating and said, 'How strange, I had a sudden conviction that you had your clothes on when I came into the bathroom last night.' He shrugged his shoulders. I ate my porridge silently.

The spell of midnight was broken but not for ever. For now the memory of midnight is strange once again. We may seek to dispel it with nightclubs or late-night cinemas, but the true flavour of midnight is in the emptiness and the grey silence of that town without its people.

Sinead Cusack

We were going to see 'Star Wars' – Sam and I. It was a huge treat. He was five years old and entranced by all things galactic and strange. We were having a shower together, I remember, in preparation for our outing and he was bombarding me with soapy questions about the film:

'And who plays the bad one Mummy, Darth Vader, who plays him?'

'I don't know darling, I can't remember the actor's name.'

'Is it Mrs Thatcher, Mummy?' he blithely asked!

Brian Matthew

'Out of the mouths . . .'

I am passionately devoted to sailing. It's not so much a hobby, more a way of life away from work. And it all began because of a little boy.

Many years ago, my wife and I took our son Christopher, then aged about five, to the Boat Show at Earl's Court. Considering the state of our finances at the time, the purpose of the visit was to gawp and covet rather than to purchase.

We duly gawped, and I certainly coveted, while Christopher trotted along uncharacteristically quietly in our wake.

We left the show and began our walk back to the car park. Without warning, Chris suddenly stopped in his tracks, his face crumpled and he burst into floods of tears.

'What's the matter?' we asked.

'It's stupid!' he blubbed, 'Whoever heard of anybody going to the Boat Show and not buying a boat?'

We went back the next day and bought one.

More than twenty-five years later, we're now on our sixth boat, and Chris lives on his.

Peter Nichols

When my eldest child, Louise, was eight or so, I came into the bathroom one day to find her tearing apart a daisy chain she'd made in the garden and throwing the flowers one by one down the lavatory.

'There,' she said.

'What's the idea?'

'Now Angela's dad will see those daisies.'

'How?'

'Because he works down the sewers, doesn't he?'

'Angela Dunn's dad?'

'No,' she snapped back, 'Angela Kirkham's!'

'All right, don't bite my head off.'

'Well, honestly. Angela Dunn's dad doesn't go down the sewers. He's got enough to do up here looking after her.'

Diana Rigg

My daughter had a disarming habit of disclaiming responsibility whenever a major spillage happened.

'Mummy, that was an acc-I-didn't.'

She was about four at the time.

Jilly Cooper

December 17th 1977

A walk with both children (Felix aged nine, Emily aged six). They have a long discussion about how old I'll be when they're both seventy.

Emily says: 'You'll be over 100, Mummy, and paralysed, and you'll have lost all your legs and arms.'

Felix thinks and then says: 'You might not, if you use Oil of Ulay.'

Felix then says he loves me more than anything in the world, then on reflection adds truthfully: 'Except television.'

I feel this is a very high compliment.

From *The Common Years* (Methuen, London).

Frank Williams

I never cease to be amazed at how much information children can take in, retain – and then produce when you are least expecting it. A few years ago I was conducting a weekend meeting at my house with a very high-powered executive. My six-year-old son, Jonathan, was playing nearby and seemed to be in a world of his own. A car-orientated world, it must be said, for there were toy cars strewn over the carpet, but it was his own world; of that we were sure.

We were at a crucial stage of the business discussions and my guest was asking me why one of our cars, driven by Alan Jones, had had an unfortunate run of mechanical failures.

'He had a lot of electrical problems and the water pump went at Silverstone,' said a tiny voice from the carpet. We both broke into laughter – and I went on to conclude a very worthwhile sponsorship deal.

Bryan Robson

Claire, aged six, and Charlotte, aged four, were sitting doing their school homework. I overheard Charlotte saying, 'I can't read these small letters.'

Claire, being a very concerned sister asked, 'Is there anything wrong with your eyes?'

To which Charlotte replied, 'No, I can't read the big letters either.'

Leo McKern

Jane was washing up, I was working and not there, the kitchen window was opened on to the side passage of our flat, and it was summer.

Abigail was about six, and playing outside with a next door friend. They had obviously exhausted the possibilities of what they were doing and the following conversation ensued, starting with the old favourite question dreaded by parents the world over.

Abigail: 'What'll we do now?'
Friend: 'I don't know.'
Abigail: 'What about shopping?'
Friend: 'No, that's no good – what about models?'
Abigail: 'We'd have to get clothes and that'd be a nuisance. What about the Queen in the tower?'
Friend: 'Oh yes, good – I'll be the Queen and you be the knight who saves me.'
Abigail: 'Don't be silly – God saves the Queen – I'll save the baby.'

Marti Caine

At a pre-Christmas parents' evening at my younger son's school, nativity paintings adorned the walls of the five-year-olds' classroom. Max's painting looked like this:

Max proclaimed proudly, 'I painted that picture of Round John Virgin, Mother and Child!'

Angela Thorne

One Christmas morning a few years ago we were all in church. It was a large gathering of the family, some of whom had travelled some distance to be with us in London. We took up two pews and the church was packed, and the procession of choirboys and girls, men and women lay preachers, etc., were passing down the centre aisle. My youngest son, Laurie, aged four was standing on the aisle next to his grandfather. The vicar was dressed in his cloak of gold looking very splendid and as he passed Laurie and my father, Laurie announced in a loud voice to the family, '*He* is Jesus's Best Friend!'

Jan Leeming

Here are some lines that my son and his friends have come out with in the car on their way home from school:

Mark: 'God must have awfully long arms.'
Me: 'Why?'
Mark: 'Well, when you die God reaches down and takes you up to Heaven and then has to put the mud back.'
Jonathan (my son): 'No, no, when you go to Heaven you leave the box behind.'

Friend: 'Do you think God can fly?'
Second friend: 'Of course not, silly.'
Jonathan: 'Of course he can, he's just like Superman.'

The Rt. Hon. Cecil Parkinson
Member of Parliament

When my daughter, Joanna, was five years old we took her to London to show her Buckingham Palace and the

Houses of Parliament and various other places of interest. As we drove down The Mall from Trafalgar Square towards Buckingham Palace, I pointed out to her the Queen Mother's home, Clarence House, which, as you know, is a very beautiful and imposing residence. Joanna was quite shaken that it was neither a Castle nor a Palace and, shaking her head, said rather sadly, 'Daddy it is very unfair on the Queen Mother that she has to live in a semi-detached house' – some semi-detached, some House!

John Conteh

My daughter Joanna, who is seven years of age, said something to me the other day which, the more I thought about it, the more hilarious it became. She had asked myself and my wife what raped meant, apparently she had heard the word off television as part of the news. After trying to explain to her she said 'Oh, I thought he meant that the woman had been raked with a garden rake.' My wife and I smiled at her and I thought how innocently children interpret the information given out by adults.

Maureen Lipman

Childspoofs

After *How was it for you?* I received a complaint from
one reviewer about including cute sayings from the
mouths of my babes and chucklings. I never thought of
my kids as 'cute'. Acute maybe. Eccentric, certainly. If
ever I doubted that, confirmation came one hot summer's
day when I found them sitting on the hall stairs wearing
man-sized wellington boots, woolly hats, scarves and
gloves, fishing with twigs and twine in a bucket of water
for a plastic lobster and a plastic crab. This would have
been normal enough, had they not been singing in
unison, in very slow dirge-like voices, 'There's no business like show business'.

Or the time when they announced they were leaving
home after some dread confrontation regarding the trim-
ming of fringes or the losing of more than one anorak a
term. 'Adam and I are going to leave home,' announced
Amy, furiously packing furry animals into a tote bag.
'We're going to dig a hole and live in it. But,' she said,
interrupting the derisory expression I was about to
assume, 'it will be a *detailed* hole.' I knew what she
meant. I've been living in a detailed hole for years – I'm
still trying to dig my way out of it.

My son is an obsessive creature and his current
obsession is astronomy. His knowledge of the workings
of the universe turn me into glazed chintz within two
minutes of his engaging my interest. A free telescope

was dispatched at enormous expense from kindly friends in Massachusetts, and binoculars purchased to tide him over the wait. The first night as a binoculars owner was spent in a deck chair in the garden gazing at the moon. He was there for hours making the kind of noises Christopher Columbus must have made when confronted by the Statue of Liberty. 'My God!' he cried. 'I've got an incredible terrain! Pfwah! I can see everything!' He was beside himself with excitement. 'The Sea of Tranquillity – yes, look – I've got it!' It was only after three hours and a faint drizzle that we discovered his binoculars were trained on next door's florescent garden light.

My kids' knowledge of the facts of life have fortunately not been any of my responsibility. Any time I tried to broach the subject I was told to knock it off in no uncertain terms and would I please not embarrass them further. This puzzled me at first. I never had a sex education as such – I mean, I knew from the girls at school roughly what went on, and could laugh and crack jokes along with the most ribald of them. But I was a good nineteen (very good) before I actually *believed* it! I swore then and there that my children would be enlightened from an early age. Frank, open discussions around the family table. Full access to our bedroom and bathroom and all unspeakable questions answered with a story, a hymn and aplomb.

Wrong again. They don't want this. 'Mo-o-od – can we change the subject, please? Look, we don't want to *know* – I mean, we know – ssssh – it's *The Colbys*.'

The Colbys. Dynasty. If there's a finger worth pointing it's in the direction of those oil-filled oleogarchies. 'Who's that?' I say as yet another wide-boned smoothy oozes blandness across a 'Le Mirage' table.

'Oh, that's Adam,' murmurs my enlightened eleven-year-old. 'He's her brother-in-law. He raped Jeff's old wife and now he's pining the blame on Stephen, but he's gay. That's his boyfriend, Luke, anyway it's not the same actress playing Fallon . . . Oh, yucky kissing, don't look!'

'Why is she having breakfast with him if he raped her? How do you know about rape? I mean, do you understand the seriousness of it?'

'Shhh, Alexis is undoing Dex's trousers again – urgh, yuck, geroff – I'm not looking . . .'

I used to adore Susan Harris's *Soap* because it went as far as your imagination's boundaries could travel and was screamingly funny along the way. Will you ever forget Jody telling Jessica he was gay, and her despondent question as to why so many people had suddenly decided to be homosexuals? Jody says, 'No, Mom – there have always been gay people throughout history. Socrates was gay, Homer was gay, Plato was gay.'

'Plato was gay?' Jessica interrupts. 'I don't *believe* it.'

'S'true,' insists Jody. 'Everyone knows that.'

'*Plato* was gay? Plato was *gay*? No – no, I can't handle this.'

'Mom, I'm telling you, Plato was – '

Jessica's eyes are popping. 'Plato gay? You're telling me Mickey Mouse's *dog* was gay?'

Crazy, yes. Funny, certainly. Ironic – the show had real irony. Something most Americans can't even pronounce. So what do they do? They take it off the air on grounds of 'moral indecency', leaving the field open to Dex's bulging trousers, Alexis's heaving upper lip, and lines like 'You wrapped her in dreams. Your dreams tried to make her in your image' and 'I'm trying to leave a failed marriage with as much dignity as I can muster.'

What worries me is that our kids are learning the fiction of life not the facts from the television programmes they choose to watch.

'Why do you watch this rubbish?' I asked them, knowing that to ban it would make it more tempting.

'Because it's so terrible,' said Amy. 'Besides, we always close our eyes and sing when they start doing yucky kissing things.'

But they don't.

Recently I came back from New York and told the family about a newspaper report concerning a demonstration against Reagan's Aids policy. There were, of course, many homosexuals among the protesters and apparently the police had been issued with yellow rubber gloves to wear for the occasion. We were laughing about this when Amy spoke out in a puzzled sort of way. 'But I don't understand. Are homosexuals afraid of yellow?'

It's the logic of children's response to our mode of speech which intrigues me. And it's not just children who respond in a child-like way. There was a recent report in *The Telegraph* about a girl assistant in a jewellery shop, selling a cross to a customer. 'Which sort did you want to look at, sir?' she enquired. 'We've got the plain silver, the plain gold, and the patterned gold. Oh, and we've got some others with a little man on.' A little man! Two thousand years of solid symbolism and it's come to that.

Or take the conversation recorded on a bus in 1959 and exhumed for the BBC radio programme, *When Housewives Had the Choice*, in 1987. Two women on a bus, one showing the other family snaps.

'That doesn't look a bit like your Brian.'

1st Woman: 'It's not our Brian.'

153

'Isn't it? Well I never, it looks just like him.'

1st Woman: 'But you just said it looked nothing like him.'

'No, well, I meant it doesn't look like him if it is him, but if it isn't it does.'

Maybe one of the things I felt I had in common with the late great Joyce Grenfell was her obsessive people-watching. It's also Alan Bennett's and Victoria Wood's great occupation, and we can overhear their overhearing in the dialogue they write. Joyce once overheard one waitress whispering to another as they came through the revolving doors from the kitchen: 'Well, he's *eaten* it!'

Many years and the Irish Sea between us, I was filming *Educating Rita* in Dublin and an extra line of dialogue was called for in a waitressing scene. Director Lewis Gilbert suggested I walk up to Julie Waters and whisper darkly, 'Well, he's eaten it!' Could Joyce Grenfell and Lewis Gilbert have eaten in the same restaurant, or is that line and all that it implies the most common of restaurant parlance? I suspect the latter. Restaurants breed good dialogue, as in 'Waitress, I want a coffee, without cream.' *Waitress*: 'We haven't got any cream, so you'll have to have it without milk.'

Still on a culinary note, Adam and his two friends, David and Daniel – sounds like something out of *Genesis*, I know, but very trendy round these parts – the Bible Belt, we call it – it came to pass that they were discussing school dinners. Adam mentioned something that David hadn't eaten at lunchtime, and, contrary to the empty plate rule, had got away with it. Daniel sprang to David's defence. 'He *can't* eat it, stupid!' he bellowed. 'He's allergic to adjectives!' So is my publisher, funnily enough.

154

Or, straight out of Luke, I give you Matthew, aged six, who is my dresser's godson. 'Mummy, don't think I'm being economical with the truth, but you really are the most cleanest loveliest mother a baby boy could ever have.' Now, if one of mine had said that I'd have had it cross-stitched on to a sampler and hung for life in a place guaranteed to embarrass the bum off him when he brought home his first girlfriend or boyfriend. Or laptop desk module, with meaningful interface and floppy discs. Whatever the 1990s equivalent is – I'm ready. Loins akimbo, shoulders girded, chin receding, teeth out, breasts plated (not to mention deflated), and mind so *open* you can hear the wind coming through the wry.

NB I've just found a note from my daughter who I now think is writing for posterity. It says:

'Hello friendly Mom and Dad!

We had a yummy Chinois (or slitty-eyed meal as Prince Philip would say), didn't we?

What shall we call the new word-processor? How about Marguerite? Cute, eh?

Thanks for a jolly existence. Love, Trog.

I blame the father. Whoever he is.

From *Something To Fall Back On* (Robson Books Ltd).

Janet Ellis

My daughter, Sophie, when aged five was being per- suaded by my mother to give up her habit of sucking her fingers to get to sleep. '*I* sucked my *thumb*,' said my mother, 'but I stopped – if you make a huge effort, you can break a habit, you know.' Sophie stared piercingly at her grandmother. 'You stopped sucking *your* thumb?' she enquired.

'Absolutely,' replied my mother. 'Grandma' replied Sophie, 'was that when you took up smoking?'

Lulu

I found this little note from Jordan when John was away.

Mammy I am
slepping in your

bed because I
felt a bit
Lonely
Jordan

Hanna Corbishley

National Secretary of The National Childbirth Trust

My son Tom's birthday is at the end of November. In 1960 he was three and in those days they switched on the Christmas lights in Oxford and Regent Streets at about this time. They were particularly spectacular and we decided to take Tommy for a ride on top of a bus to see them. He was entranced. As we got off, he turned to me in wonderment: 'How did they know it was my birthday?' he said. And of course he was quite right; the world was made just for him.

Ian Beer

Headmaster, Harrow School

The whole family were sitting round for Sunday lunch with the roast beef just placed on the table. One of the three young children was asked by mummy to say grace for the family and just as the grace was about to be uttered the telephone bell rang . . . the lazy daddy requested the same poor child to answer the telephone and on picking up the receiver he was heard to say in a loud voice, 'For what we are about to receive may the Lord make us truly grateful!'

Topol

We had a kitchen, bathroom and toilet, all of which we shared with the four members of the Eisenberg family. Mr Eisenberg was a carpenter, but presumably as successful in his craft as my father was in his, for Mrs Eisenberg also had a sewing-machine. On summer evenings when the doors and windows were open to catch any air that was about and she and my mother were bent over their respective machines, the clatter of their treadles sounded like prolonged exchanges of machine-gun fire. Her sewmanship was of a more intricate kind than my mother's, for she was principally engaged in embroidery. She also had a beautiful voice. My father too had a pleasant voice. They were both from Warsaw and shared the same fund of folk songs, which ranged from music hall songs to the anthems of the Zionist movement via Chassidic melodies, and sometimes they would sing together in the warm evenings as they sat out on adjoining balconies. She also sang as she bent over her cooking or cleaning or scrubbing though, if I look back on it, she had little to sing about. We had the right-hand side of the sink, and they had the left; we had our primus and petelia (a sort of slow-burning primus which, as far as I know, was peculiar to Israel and which could be used for baking) and they had theirs. As both she and my mother were compact little women, they did not get too much in each other's way, except when preparing for the Sabbath or holidays. On weekdays we did not eat all that much or that often, and the sort of dishes we had then did not call for prolonged vigils over the primus or petelia.

If we had no difficulties in the kitchen, there were occasional difficulties in the bathroom, for we had but the one bath to be shared among nine people and a considerable number of fish.

During weekdays, if we ate fish at all, we would make do with *dag-fillet*, which was frozen cod, but there was only one fish fit to grace a Shabbat or *Yom Tov* table and that was carp. The carp were bought fresh from a tank, rushed home thrashing and flapping, and then left free to swim in the bath till it was time for the slaughter. I don't know how mother told our carp apart from the Eisenberg carp – but come Thursday night, the water would be let out of the bath and mother would kill the fish with one whack across the head with a wooden mallet. I loved carp, but I could never bring myself to kill them or even to watch them being killed.

We normally washed in the shower, but on a Friday afternoon, with the approach of the Sabbath, especially in winter, all nine of us wanted to wash and stay clean, without getting too much in each other's way, or on each other's nerves, which suggests careful timing, and a degree of patience and good humour which would be unattainable today.

The water in the bathroom was heated by a great, groaning geyser which puffed and fumed, and which sometimes sounded as if it might take off. I once slipped while in the shower, grasped at a pipe to steady myself and brought the whole creaking apparatus crashing into the bath. I somehow escaped injury, but the occasion is recalled in our family, and perhaps among the Eisenbergs, as the dirty Sabbath, and for a time all nine of us had to wash in the sink. And yet though we washed and cooked cheek to cheek, even fish to fish, we never quarrelled and when in 1951 we moved to more spacious quarters – a three-roomed apartment in Kiryath Shalom – the Eisenbergs chose to move into the same block.

From *Topol by Topol* (Weidenfeld and Nicolson Ltd)